Rachel Burke

Be Dazzling

Simple projects to make your wardrobe sparkle

Hardie Grant

BOOKS

Contents

Introduction

Ever since I was little, I've had the urge to dunk myself in glitter. One of my earliest memories is of stuffing (to the brim!) the pockets of my pre-prep art smock with sequins, gems and pipe cleaners; I was gently asked to remove them before leaving class that day. Like a magpie, I would collect shiny things and hide them away, constantly curating my own personal treasure chest.

These treasures have always been the same things – gems, sequins, beads ... and POMPOMS! What started as a juvenile appreciation of these materials has grown into a constant, unwavering desire to adorn myself and others in these things that bring me so much joy.

For me, more is always more! I have never been one for minimalism, embracing instead a style that isn't afraid to surprise and is always ready to dazzle. The rush that comes from stepping into a room while clad in a surprising and unique outfit is something I have come to cherish – and it's an experience I'm excited to share with you all!

Understated is overrated. MORE IS MORE. Be Dazzling.

Tools and materials

RIBBON

ACRYLIC POMPOMS

PIPE CLEANERS

SEQUINS

FAKE GEMS

WASHI MASKING TAPE

HOT GLUE GUN

SHARP SCISSORS

HANDMADE POMPOMS

WOOL YARN

FUSE BEADS

FAKE PEARLS

FELT PENS

FAKE FLOWERS

TINSEL

COLOURED CARD

PAPER (CUPCAKE) CASES

Gem for joy

Making tips

- It's no surprise that gems are one of the key materials in many of the designs in this book. I find that they add a glorious garnish to almost any project, taking things from BORE to J'ADORE! As wonderful as gems are on their own, they are often made EVEN better when paired with other materials. Mix them with fake pearls, beads and other fun trinkets to give your design extra texture and spangle. You can even deconstruct old jewellery and repurpose it to tremendous effect!

- If you are covering something entirely in gems, approach the project as though you are creating a mosaic. Try to evenly space out your gems, dispersing them neatly over whatever surface you are covering. Spacing them about 5 mm (¼ in) apart is a good rule of thumb.

- Keep your eyes peeled for coloured gems at craft stores, or have a little hunt online for good bulk deals and fun colours.

- When gluing your gems, aim to dab the glue right at the centre of the gem's back, applying a small blob that's roughly 5 mm (¼ in). I don't love the look of glue spilling out around the sides of a gem and this amount keeps that from happening.

- Don't be afraid to gem-on-gem! Layering gems makes things look super lush and fabulous.

- One of the great things about hot glue is that you don't have to factor in drying time. It only takes seconds to dry and cool, which means you can gem-and-wear with ease!

Shoe-nicorns

If you need a statement pair of shoes for a fun occasion or want to make a splash on your next stroll to the shops, then I recommend creating your own pair of shoe-nicorns (i.e. shoes fit for a unicorn).

YOU WILL NEED

- 1 bottle of clear, glittery nail polish
- 1 pair of old plain-coloured boots or shoes, wiped clean
- hot glue gun
- enough gems, fuse beads and sequins to densely cover your shoes, in a variety of colours and sizes

HOW TO: SHOE-NICORNS

1.

....

Paint your shoes all over
with the glittery nail polish
and set aside for 15 minutes
to dry.

2.

....

Dab some glue onto the backs
of your gems, fuse beads and
sequins and fix them to your
shoes in a random pattern,
leaving roughly 5 mm (¼ in)
between them.

3.

....

Keep going until you have
covered your shoes entirely,
but I recommend you don't
embellish laces or zips.
Your shoes will be ready to
wear (and dazzle) as soon as
you've finished gluing!

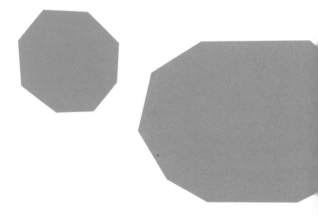

Bedazzled jacket

After a few winters, it's easy to end up with a wardrobe filled with miscellaneous jackets that perhaps you no longer wear. What better way to make an old jacket fresh again than to cover it all over with GEMS?

YOU WILL NEED

....

- 1 old jacket (or a new one, if you're into it), preferably woven or furry to help your gems stick and stay

- hot glue gun

- enough gems, fuse beads and sequins to densely cover the top half of your jacket, in a variety of colours and sizes

HOW TO: BEDAZZLED JACKET

1.

Settle down in front of one of your favourite binge-worthy TV shows. This is going to take a while.

2.

Starting at the shoulders, dab some glue on the back of a gem, fuse bead or sequin … and get gluing! Leave about 5 mm (¼ in) between each embellishment. The aim is to cover the whole upper half of the jacket with sparkle, thinning out your placement as you reach the middle of the jacket and tapering off as you reach the bottom. This will make it look like your shiny bits are cascading down the garment, which I think is quite lovely.

Gem funglasses

The eyes are the window to the soul and should be adorned with enough razzle-dazzle to appropriately reflect your inner FABULOUSNESS.

YOU WILL NEED

· 1 pair of glasses or sunglasses (I used pink-lensed sunglasses)

· hot glue gun

· about 32 teardrop-shaped crystal gems

· about 33 small circular crystal gems

· about 8 small circular pink and mauve gems

1.

Squeeze some glue onto the back of a teardrop gem (its wide bottom, not its pointy top) and fix it to an upper corner of your frames. From there, glue more teardrops across the top of your frames, leaving no space in between them.

2.

Glue a second layer of teardrops on top of the first, placing them just off centre so they cover the places where the first line of gems touch. This will make your glasses look extra lush.

3.

Glue the small circular crystal gems to the curved bottom half of your frames, leaving no space in between them.

4.

Glue a light smattering of pink and mauve gems around the curved bottom half of your frames on top of the first layer. Now pop them on and get ready to dazzle!

Gem flower brooch

Ever wanted to tell a pal 'great job!' but couldn't quite find the right way to say it? Ever had a top that needed a little bit of extra *je ne sais quoi*? Well, this flower brooch is here to help. Make a few and pin them in a cluster for maximum impact. Don't be afraid to experiment with flower placement and how many embellishments you use! With this project, the sky's the limit.

YOU WILL NEED

- 5 cm (2 in) scalloped circle punch or scissors
- 1 sheet of coloured card
- hot glue gun
- 1 sequin flower
- 5-10 teardrop-shaped gems
- 5-10 small or medium circular gems
- scissors
- 10 cm (4 in) length of ribbon
- 1 badge back

HOW TO: GEM FLOWER BROOCH

1.

Using your circle punch, cut a circle out of the card: this will be your brooch's base. If you don't have a circle punch, you can just use scissors. (The size of your base will dictate the final size of your brooch, so feel free to make it bigger if you want it to be flashy.)

2.

Glue the sequin flower and gems to your base. Feel free to experiment with placement here: for a balanced look, glue the flower to the centre of your base, then surround it with gems.

3.

Snip a small triangle out of one end of the ribbon. Glue the un-snipped end to the back of your base.

4.

Glue the badge back onto the back of your brooch.

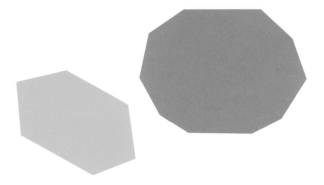

Bedazzled collar

Have a few old collared shirts lying about? Need to add some fun to your neckline? Well, get out the hot glue gun and transform a humble collar into a dazzling work of art. Wear it over the collar of your favourite shirt, tee, or on its own as a fabulous neckpiece!

YOU WILL NEED

· 1 old collared shirt

· scissors

· hot glue gun

· enough gems, fuse beads
  and sequins to cover
  your collar, in a variety
  of colours and sizes

HOW TO: BEDAZZLED COLLAR

1.

Unbutton the shirt and cut the collar off just under the neck seam. Make sure you cut underneath the top button panel so the collar can still be buttoned up when you're done.

2.

Glue your gems, fuse beads and sequins onto the outside of the collar. Place them so they're facing in all different directions, making sure they're quite close together so the finished collar is entirely encrusted in bedazzlement. Don't be afraid to layer as you go!

Gem earrings

These earrings never fail to brighten up an outfit, so I prefer to call them 'cheerings'! I like this colour combo, but feel free to branch out and experiment with others.

YOU WILL NEED

- two 20 cm (8 in) lengths of floristry wire (about 1 mm thick)
- 2 earring hooks
- wire cutter
- hot glue gun
- 14 teardrop-shaped crystal gems
- 12 fake pearls
- 14 small circular green gems
- about 30 large circular blue gems

HOW TO: GEM EARRINGS

1.

Coil each strand of wire into a circle, then squeeze them gently until they look like ovals.

2.

Thread one earring hook onto one end of wire, then secure it by twisting the two ends of the wire together, closing up your oval shape. Keep twisting the wire until it feels secure, then trim off any excess. Don't be alarmed if it looks a little unsightly – it will soon be entirely covered with gems!

3.

Put a generous dab of glue on the back of a teardrop gem (at its pointy end), then glue it onto the wide bottom of one of the wire ovals. Add six more teardrops, making sure there's no space in between them.

4.

Glue six pearls on top of the teardrops at their pointy ends. Make sure not to leave any space between them.

5.

Glue green gems on top of each teardrop at its rounded end.

6.

Glue half of the blue gems to the remaining bare wire, using overlapping layers to fill in any gaps and give the design some depth.

7.

Repeat steps 2 through 6 with the other wire oval and get ready to sparkle!

Tinsel town

Making tips

- When decorating something with tinsel, I like to start at the bottom and move my way up to the top. It means you don't have to glue underneath any lines of tinsel, which often leads to gluing strands together by mistake!

- When gluing tinsel onto both sides of a garment, put a towel or old T-shirt in between the layers to avoid them sticking together as you glue.

- Where possible, use tinsel that is sold in a strip (often called lametta). This will make it so much easier to glue or sew it to your garment. If you use loose strands, you may encounter a tinsel nightmare!

- To join tinsel lametta strips together, just use a stapler! You can always glue a little tinsel down over the staple to cover it up.

- If you don't like the idea of gluing tinsel onto your garment, you can try your hand at whizzing the tinsel through the sewing machine instead.

- I generally use three different types of tinsel: flat-fringed lametta strips, skinny-fringed lametta strips and normal, Christmas-style tinsel. Flat-fringed and skinny-fringed strips are great options for applying to clothing, and you can use either for the designs in this chapter. Christmas-style tinsel is better for snipping up and using as small embellishments and accessories. For projects such as the tinsel dress (page 38) and rainbow tinsel jacket (page 41), the cheerleader pompom tinsel packs you'll find at dollar shops are perfecto.

Tinsel-shoulder T-shirt

Cold shoulders are a thing of the past with this nifty project! Needless to say, this piece is perfect for shimmying, and it's a great way to use up thin tinsel strips. Try to use tinsel that's 25 cm (10 in) long to ensure it drapes nicely down your arms and encourages twirling!

YOU WILL NEED

· tape measure

· 1 old, plain T-shirt
  (or new, if you're into it)

· scissors

· 2 m (6½ ft) tinsel lametta
  strips (I used silver, but
  any colour will do)

· hot glue gun

HOW TO: TINSEL-SHOULDER T-SHIRT

1.

....

Measure the circumference
of one of your T-shirt's
sleeves, then cut your tinsel
strips to that length. Cutting
the tinsel to size will make
it easier to glue on - and less
likely to stick to itself as
you go.

2.

....

Squeeze a line of glue onto
the back of a tinsel strip.
Press the tinsel to the
hemline (bottom edge) of
your sleeve until it wraps
all the way around.

3.

....

Repeat this process up the
sleeve, leaving approximately
4 cm (1½ in) between each strip
and stopping when you reach the
shoulder seam (the top of the
sleeve where the stitching is).

4.

....

Repeat steps 1 through 3 on
your other sleeve until you're
bedecked in glorious layers
of tinsel.

Tinsel skirt

This project has saved me on more than one occasion! It is such a ritzy (and easy) way to complete a fun outfit ... and best of all, it is PERFECT for twirling.

YOU WILL NEED

....

- 2 m (6½ ft) length of ribbon, approximately 10 cm (4 in) thick

- measuring tape

- scissors

- 2 m (6½ ft) of tinsel lametta strips (approximately 45 cm/1½ ft long)

- felt pen

- sewing machine

- thread

HOW TO: TINSEL SKIRT

1.

Wrap the ribbon around your waist. Add on an extra 60 cm (2 ft) to that length and cut the ribbon. Using your felt pen, make a small mark 20 cm (8 in) in from both ends of the ribbon to indicate the area onto which you'll sew your tinsel.

2.

Cut the tinsel into six 30 cm (1 ft) strips, discarding any excess.

3.

Lay your ribbon down on the bed of your sewing machine, lining one of the small marks up with the needle. Lay a strip of tinsel on top of the ribbon at its bottom edge, making sure to line its end up with the first mark. Using a basic top stitch, sew back and forth for a few stitches to make sure your tinsel is securely fastened, then sew until you reach the second mark. Sew backwards for a few stitches to secure it, then cut the string.

4.

Repeat step 3 with the remaining tinsel strips, sewing them onto your ribbon in layers (to build up the thickness) until the skirt is looking lush.

5.

Use the bare ends of ribbon to tie on your skirt. I recommend angling the bow to the back or side of your body, and REALLY recommend wearing a pair of bike pants, shorts or a miniskirt underneath to avoid an unwanted 'flashy affair'!

Tinsel dress

How can you resist the lure of being decked out entirely in tinsel? The answer is that you can't. You simply can't, so don't fight it. Get ready to upcycle an old frock and turn it into a fabulous glitter ball!

YOU WILL NEED

· about 10 m (33 ft) of tinsel lametta strips in a variety of colours

· tape measure

· scissors

· 1 old dress (ideally cotton or woven)

· hot glue gun

HOW TO: TINSEL DRESS

1.

Cut your tinsel strips into 20 cm (8 in) pieces. This will make them more manageable to attach to your dress.

2.

Lay your dress out flat. Squeeze a line of glue onto the back of a tinsel strip and attach it 20 cm (8 in) above the hemline (bottom edge) – you want to make sure the tinsel overhangs by at least 3 cm (1¼ in). Continue gluing strips of tinsel in a line around your dress, alternating colours as you go.

3.

Measure 20 cm (8 in) up from the first line of tinsel and repeat step 2, creating another wraparound layer. Continue gluing on layers of tinsel until you get to the neckline.

4.

Glue strips of tinsel to the upper half of your dress, across the shoulder seams, collar and the upper back.

5.

For maximum impact, glue some extra tinsel at the top of the shoulders and over any lametta strip edges that might be peeking out from the design.

Rainbow tinsel jacket

There is nothing quite like taking an old, forgotten garment and turning it into a show-stopping piece that you will want to wear again and again. Enjoy the sensation of feeling like a human rainbow!

YOU WILL NEED

· 1 old blazer or denim jacket

· scissors

· about 5 m (16 ft) of tinsel lametta strips in a variety of colours

· hot glue gun

HOW TO: RAINBOW TINSEL JACKET

1.

Cut the sleeves of your jacket to shorten them to T-shirt length.

2.

Cut your tinsel strips into 20 cm (8 in) pieces. This will make them more manageable to attach to your jacket.

3.

Lay your jacket out flat. Squeeze a line of glue onto the back of a tinsel strip and attach it 10 cm (4 in) up from the hemline (bottom edge). Continue this process all the way around the garment, alternating colours as you go.

4.

Measure 10 cm (4 in) up from your first line of tinsel and repeat step 2, creating another wraparound layer. Continue gluing on layers of tinsel until you get to the jacket's neckline.

5.

Glue strips of tinsel to the upper half of the jacket, across the shoulder seams, collar and the upper back.

6.

Glue strips of tinsel onto the hemline (bottom edge) of your sleeves, working up to the shoulder seam. To ensure your sleeves are extra lush, I recommend three or four layers on each sleeve.

7.

Once your jacket is completely covered, feel free to trim some of the tinsel to create choppy layers and expose different colours. Play around with it to achieve your desired effect.

Flamenco pink jacket

For some reason, over the years I have amassed a collection of raffia skirts (you know, those ones you get at bargain shops for last-minute Halloween costume emergencies). Not wanting to waste my rather impressive collection, I decided to transform them into a statement piece to wear anytime of the year.

YOU WILL NEED

· 4 pink raffia skirts (with a drape of about 38 cm/15 in)

· scissors

· 1 old denim jacket

· hot glue gun

HOW TO: FLAMENCO PINK JACKET

1.

Prep your raffia skirts by plucking off any fake flowers and chopping off or unpicking any Velcro panels. Cut them into 30 cm (1 ft) strips to make the raffia easier to work with.

2.

Cut the sleeves of your jacket to shorten them to T-shirt length.

3.

Lay your jacket out flat. Squeeze a line of glue onto the back of a raffia strip and attach it halfway up the front of the jacket. Continue this process all the way around the garment.

4.

Repeat step 2 with another strip of raffia, creating another wraparound layer 20 cm (8 in) above the first. Continue gluing on layers of raffia until you reach the jacket's neckline.

5.

Attach raffia strips to the upper half of the jacket, gluing across the shoulder seams, collar and back. You should only need three layers of raffia to cover the whole thing.

6.

Glue raffia strips onto the hemline (bottom edge) of your sleeves, working your way up to the shoulder seam in layers. To ensure your sleeves are extra lush, I recommend three to four layers per sleeve.

Shoe clips

Why not complete your most tinsel-perfect outfit with a matching pair of sparkling shoes? This speedy trick is oh-so-fabulous and allows you to reinvent a humble pair of shoes in minutes.

YOU WILL NEED

· scissors

· measuring tape

· 1 sheet of coloured card

· hot glue gun

· 2 standard bobby pins

· two 10 cm (4 in) tinsel lametta strips in whatever colour you fancy

HOW TO: SHOE CLIPS

1.

Cut two circles out of the card, each roughly 10 cm (4 in) in diameter.

2.

Squeeze a dab of glue onto the centre of one of your circles and press the top of a bobby pin into it. This will be the bottom of your shoe clip.

3.

Pinch a strip of tinsel into a ball. Squeeze some glue onto the top of your card circle and press down your ball of tinsel. Hold it down with some pressure for a few seconds, which should prevent the tinsel from slipping or the glue from moving around as it dries.

4.

Repeat steps 1 through 3 to create your second shoe clip.

5.

Slide your finished clips onto the tongues of your shoes. If you're attaching them to sneakers, secure the pin to the shoelace section.

Pipe cleaner crown

Why wait to be ordained when you can crown yourself a kween any old day of the week? This project urges you to choose your own adventure and customise a crown to your liking. Use whatever colours and design you like!

YOU WILL NEED

- measuring tape
- about 8 metallic pipe cleaners in a single colour (I used purple)
- about 3 metallic silver pipe cleaners in a different colour (I used silver)
- hot glue gun
- a smattering of gems, pompoms, beads and tinsel scraps

HOW TO: PIPE CLEANER CROWN

1.

Wrap the measuring tape around your head, right where you want your crown to sit, and note the circumference.

2.

Create a length of pipe cleaners with the same circumference as your head. Twist their ends together to form a circle, then push the circle down on your head to shape the base of your crown.

3.

Bend five pipe cleaners of a particular colour (I used purple) in half, creating a bunch of triangles. Connect them to the base of your crown by twisting their ends around it until they feel secure. I like to overlap them for added interest and put the largest triangle right at the front. You can keep the triangles contained or extend them all the way around!

4.

Bend three pipe cleaners of a different colour into various-sized ovals (I made one large, with its ends overlapping, and two small). Attach them to your triangles in whatever pattern you fancy, twisting their ends until they feel secure.

5.

Decorate your crown with tinsel sprigs, gluing them down wherever you like. Glue on some pompoms, gems, beads and any other goodies. I added a few gems and pearls to my triangles and ovals, and a few layers of gems at the base for extra dazzle.

Lovely legs

Making tips

- Bare legs can get boring. I say it's time to bedazzle them! Don't be fooled by this LOVELY leg illusion: all of these pins are actually covered in a pair of sheer tights. Once you have the method down (pages 56–7), you will find that it's easy to customise them in any way your heart desires.

- The numbers of gems, beads, etc. you'll need for each pair of tights is going to depend on what design you want to make and how lush you want it to be. Try to visualise the pattern before you get started to make sure you have enough dazzle on hand.

- You can expect the tights to stretch when you put them on, expanding the space between your decorations. If you don't want any gaps in your design for, say, a flowery pair of tights, I recommend gluing some petals together as you go.

- If you don't like the idea of gluing things to your tights, sewing works too!

Making lovely legs tights

YOU WILL NEED

- 1 pair of sheer tights
- 40 cm (16 in) cardboard or plastic tube
- hot glue gun
- enough fake flowers, gems, pompoms, bows, etc. to cover your chosen section of tights

1 PREPARE THE TIGHTS

I recommend trying your tights on before getting started, identifying where the front is and what area you want to decorate. When you roll them off, make sure to keep track of the front-facing area.

Roll one leg of your tights onto your tube. It doesn't have to be pulled tight, but having it stretched out as you decorate will be more indicative of the final result, so it can be helpful to use a thick piece of tubing.

2 GLUE DOWN DECORATIONS

Dab a bit of glue onto the back of your chosen decoration, then fix it to the tights where you'd like your design to stop (toward the top of your feet or higher up on your shins). Don't use too much glue: just a light amount will do (we don't want the tights getting stuck to the roll). Try to leave a 1 cm (½ in) gap in between each embellishment.

3 COVER THE LEG

....

Keep gluing on decorations,
moving your way up the leg,
until you've covered the tights
to your liking. Sliding your
tubing around as you move from
section to section will ensure
you cover a good-sized portion.
If this gets annoying, you can
use a longer length of tube
(like a wrapping paper roll)
or even an old length of pipe.

4 PEEL OFF

....

Peel the decorated leg off
the tube. Don't panic if some
of your materials have glued
to the roll: just be gentle,
plucking them off as you go.

5 REPEAT

....

Repeat steps 1 through 4 with
the other leg of your tights.

Flower tights

YOU WILL NEED

· 1 pair of sheer tights

· 1 cardboard or plastic tube

· hot glue gun

· 30-40 fake pink flowers, stems cut off

· a handful of gems

ARRANGING YOUR FLOWERS

Work out where you would like your floral design to stop, and begin gluing down flowers at that point. If your flower has a bit of plastic on the base, apply the glue to this section; if not, just glue down the flattest part of the flower. Keep gluing your way up the leg until you reach the point where you want your design to begin. Glue a light smattering of gems to the flower petals and to the tights themselves.

Pompom tights

YOU WILL NEED

· 1 pair of sheer tights

· 1 cardboard or plastic tube

· hot glue gun

· about 100 acrylic pompoms in a variety of colours

ARRANGING YOUR POMPOMS

Work out where you would like your pompom design to stop, and begin gluing down pompoms at that point. Alternate the colours of the pompoms as you glue your way up the tights, ensuring you glue them quite close together for a compact design. Keep gluing your way up the tights until you reach the point where you would like your design to begin.

Bow tights

YOU WILL NEED

- 1 pair of sheer tights
- 1 cardboard or plastic tube
- hot glue gun
- 50-60 fabric bows in three different colours

ARRANGING YOUR BOWS

Work out where you would like your bow design to stop, and begin gluing down bows at that point. Repeat this step until you've glued down a healthy smattering of bows!

Sequin tights

YOU WILL NEED

- 1 pair of sheer tights
- 1 cardboard or plastic tube
- hot glue gun
- at least 300 sequins in a mix of five colours
- at least 300 fuse beads in the same mix of five colours as the sequins

ARRANGING YOUR SEQUINS

Work out where you would like your sequin design to stop, and begin gluing down sequins at that point. Glue down same-coloured sequins and fuse beads, making a colour block that's roughly 20 cm (8 in) wide. Mixing fuse beads in with your sequins creates a bit of extra texture, which I find reaps lovely rewards! Add on other colour blocks to your liking. Don't worry about it being perfect - it looks better when the placement is quite free.

Gem tights

YOU WILL NEED

- 1 pair of sheer tights
- 1 cardboard or plastic tube
- hot glue gun
- about 80 gems in a variety of colours and sizes
- about 50 sequins in a variety of colours and sizes

ARRANGING YOUR GEMS

Work out where you would like your gem design to stop, and begin gluing down gems at that point. Glue as many gems and sequins onto the front of your tights as you like. Experiment with gluing the materials close together or far apart.

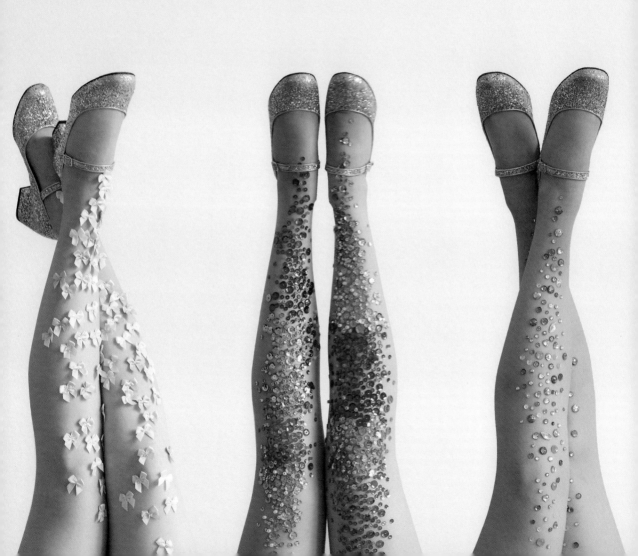

Making tips

- The bigger your pompom template is, the bigger your finished pompom will be. I like to make my pompoms in three general sizes: large (tennis ball-sized); medium (lime-sized); and small (golf ball-sized). A pompom template that is 18 cm (7 in) in diameter makes a large pompom; a template 12 cm (4¾ in) in diameter makes a medium pompom; and a template 8 cm (3¼ in) in diameter makes a small pompom.

- The more wool yarn you use while wrapping your pompom, the denser and more lush it will be.

- If you want to speed up the process of making your pompom, you can split a ball of wool and wind multiple pieces of wool at a time.

- Don't be afraid to use lots of different wool colours in your pompom. Creating multicoloured poms is as easy as SNIPping and STARTing a new colour.

- The more wool you trim off your finished pompom, the plusher it will be. If you don't trim it, it will be shaggy. Choose your own adventure here! You can use the offcuts from trimming your pompoms for other fun projects like collaging, sewing them onto the hemline of a jacket, or filling up jars with them to create colourful ornaments.

Making the perfect pompom, Rachel Burke-style

YOU WILL NEED

· 1 sheet of card
· measuring tape
· felt pen
· scissors
· 1 ball of wool yarn
  or multiple small balls
  in various colours

1 CREATE A TEMPLATE

To make a medium pompom, fold a piece of card in half, then sketch a circle onto it that's 12 cm (4¾ in) in diameter. Use the bottom of a can or glass to trace your circle if freehand is a little daunting. Cut out the circle (you'll end up with two) and stack them. Sketch a 3 cm (1¼ in)-wide keyhole onto your template – the top half of the keyhole should be at the centre, with the wide bottom half trailing off one edge – and cut it out. Your finished template should look like a doughnut with a bite-sized slice missing.

2 SPLIT THE WOOL

Split a ball of wool yarn into two balls. Winding with multiple strands of wool at a time will make your pompom come together SO much more quickly than if you were working with one strand. Using your finger, hold the end of the wool down at the centre of your template (the unbitten part of the doughnut) and start winding the wool around, under and over through the keyhole.

3 WIND THE WOOL

Keep winding. If you want to change colours, just snip off the wool you're working with and start again with a new colour. As you wind, make sure to leave a 1–2 cm (½–¾ in) gap at each of the template's ends. Your pompom is ready to progress to the next phase when your template is bursting with wool ... or, for us visual folks, when it looks like a little croissant.

4 CUT AND TIE THE WOOL

Take your scissors and cut through your wool croissant along the outer edge of the template. I find this step easier when I press down with the flat of my hand. Once your strands are cut, take a long, doubled-over strand of wool and work it lengthways between the template's two layers until you reach the inner, uncut portion of wool. Pull the two ends of the strand around until they extend out of the keyhole. Tie the strand tightly in a knot at the centre of your pompom, at which point the pompom will fluff up nicely. Pull out your template.

5 TRIM YOUR POMPOM

Trim off as much or as little wool as you like. I like to trim off a lot, as I find this gives me a really dense, plush-looking pompom. The more you make, the more you will find your style!

Pompom jacket

A pompom jacket is the perfect piece to own, and it makes an INCREDIBLE gift. The first one I made was using pompoms collected at a friend's wedding. It's a sweet memento AND a fashion statement: what could possibly be better than that? I recommend making the MANY pompoms for this project over a crafternoon, or better yet host a pompom-making event with some friends.

YOU WILL NEED

· 1 old jacket

· hot glue gun

· SO MANY HANDMADE POMPOMS!
  At least 150 (the larger they
  are, the quicker it will go)

· about 100 small acrylic
  pompoms

HOW TO: POMPOM JACKET

1.

Dab some glue onto your handmade pompoms and attach them to your jacket. You want to cover the front, shoulders and back of the garment, making sure the pompoms are touching. Place some glue between the pompoms as you go to make sure the design stays compact and looks lush.

2.

Instead of covering both sleeves entirely in handmade pompoms, I prefer to glue on some acrylic ones (this not only looks cute, but also makes it easier to move your arms around). You can make these spread out or close together: your call.

Pompom party earrings

You will be so pleased to know that I have discovered the perfect cure for bare earlobes. Get ready to start so many conversations with pals about how you made these earrings, because people are going to be asking questions!

YOU WILL NEED

- 2 large handmade multicoloured pompoms
- hot glue gun
- 2 small handmade solid-coloured pompoms
- 2 matching beads
- 2 earring hooks
- 30 small fake pearls

HOW TO: POMPOM PARTY EARRINGS

1.
....

Figure out which way you would like one of your large pompoms to hang. Glue a small pompom onto the top.

2.
....

Glue the bead onto the top of the small pompom.

3.
....

Squeeze some glue into the bead's hole and stick your earring hook into it. Hold it there for a few seconds to make sure the hook is secure.

4.
....

Glue half of the pearls onto your large pompom, spacing them out evenly.

5.
....

Repeat steps 1 through 4 to make your other earring, then pop these babies into your ears!

Pompom tote bag

I prefer to have pompoms with me at all times, and having them attached to my bag makes this goal extra easy to achieve. Mixing and matching a variety of different colours will really make your bag pop!

YOU WILL NEED

- 1 old wicker bag or basket
- hot glue gun
- at least 9 large handmade multi- and solid-coloured pompoms
- 1 yarn needle
- two 20 cm (8 in) pieces of wool yarn

HOW TO: POMPOM TOTE BAG

1.

Glue seven pompoms to the outside of your wicker bag, spreading them out neatly in whatever arrangement you like.

2.

Thread your yarn needle with one of the pieces of wool, tying a knot at the end. Pierce the centre of a leftover pompom and thread it through, stopping when the knot is flush with the pompom's edge. Remove the needle and tie a knot at the long end of the string. Repeat this step with your remaining pompom.

3.

Tie the two loose pompoms you just threaded onto one of the bag's handles.

Pompom head-pièce de résistance

I like to think of a pompom headband as being like a cake topper: it's a festive decoration, for my head! Tip: if you feel like your headpiece is a little bit heavy, use some bobby pins to secure the card panel to your hair.

YOU WILL NEED

· 1 sheet of coloured card

· felt pen

· scissors

· hot glue gun

· 1 headband

· at least 9 large and medium handmade pompoms

· a handful of small and medium acrylic pompoms

HOW TO: POMPOM HEAD-PIÈCE DE RÉSISTANCE

1.

Sketch an oval onto the sheet of card - you're aiming to make it 15 cm (6 in) long. If you're struggling to draw an oval freehand, use a medium-sized can to draw two circles that overlap by roughly 4 cm (1½ in) - it will look just like a Venn diagram. Draw lines between the tops and bottoms of the circles to create your oval.

2.

Cut out your oval and glue it lengthways onto the top of your headband.

3.

Squeeze some dots of glue onto your oval and begin attaching handmade pompoms. Once you've covered your oval, glue some pompoms onto the headband itself. You can glue as many pompoms onto your headband as you want, but I usually leave approximately 15 cm (6 in) bare on both sides so it tucks neatly behind my ears.

4.

Once you have a solid base, put some dabs of glue onto the tops of the pompoms and pile on some more. Use the acrylic pompoms to fill in any gaps in your design. How high you go with your design, and how many smaller pompoms you use, is up to you!

Pompom bracelet

Remember best friend charms? As a kid, I loved gifting my pals small trinkets to let them know they were top notch. As a grownup, the ritual hasn't lost its appeal! This project is perfect for gifting to cherished ones (and making a matching one for yourself).

YOU WILL NEED

- 27 cm (10¾ in) length of floristry wire (about 1 mm thick)
- wire cutter
- about 30 beads and fuse beads
- some letter beads (how many will depend on what you want to write)
- at least 1 small handmade pompom
- 2-3 small acrylic pompoms

HOW TO: POMPOM BRACELET

1.

Wrap some wire around your
wrist, just long enough that
you can slip it on and off
without any dramas. Trim off
the excess.

2.

Thread the beads and pompoms
onto your wire in whatever
order and pattern you like,
piercing the centre of the
pompoms with the wire so they
will stay securely fastened.
Don't be afraid to thread on
some fun words or phrases
with your letter beads!
To finish the bracelet off,
twist the wire's ends together
multiple times and trim off any
excess. Make and wear multiple
bracelets for maximum impact!

Pompom necklace

I don't wear necklaces very often, but when I do I want to make a statement. Try this simple project for making a standout necklace.

YOU WILL NEED

- one 50 cm (1 ft 8 in) length of thin twine or string
- 1 yarn needle
- about 60 fuse beads in two colours
- 4 small acrylic pompoms
- 4 medium acrylic pompoms
- 1 large handmade multicoloured pompom

HOW TO: POMPOM NECKLACE

1.

Thread your string onto the yarn needle and knot it at the end, making sure to leave enough bare string that you can tie the two ends together later.

2.

Thread on fuse beads, alternating colours as you go. Keep adding fuse beads until you get to the place on your necklace where you want your pompom centrepiece to start.

3.

Thread on four acrylic pompoms in whatever order you fancy (I like to sandwich two medium ones with two smaller ones). Add the large pompom, then the remaining acrylic pompoms, following the same order as you did on the other side. Make sure to push the needle right through the middle of your pompoms so they stay put.

4.

Fill up the remaining string with alternating fuse beads, leaving a little bit of bare thread at the end.

5.

Remove the yarn needle. Tie the ends of the necklace together with a simple knot and you're done!

Making tips

- Get your hands on a nice mix of fake flowers in a variety of sizes and colours: have a peek in bargain or craft stores for these.

- Removing the stems from your fake flowers is a great way to prep them for crafting! Keep your eyes peeled for stemless fake flowers, too, as these will be big time savers.

- Don't be afraid to mix beads, sequins and pompoms into your floral designs. The more texture, the better! They look especially nice when glued onto petals.

- Keep your eyes peeled for other treasures in your life that might benefit from a little flower glorifying, as many of the techniques in this chapter can be applied to other home goods, wardrobe items and beyond!

- If you don't want to buy fake flowers, read on and try your hand at making some paper ones ...

Making paper flowers

YOU WILL NEED

· at least 4 large paper
  (cupcake) cases

· at least 4 small paper
  (cupcake) cases

1 COLLECT

Gather together a bunch of
paper cases. It's nice to
make these paper flowers
with cases in different
sizes, colours and patterns.

2 FOLD

Fold a paper case in half,
then in half again. It should
look like a very flat slice
of pizza.

3 TWIST

Tightly twist the pointed end of the case around a few times. The other end should get fluffy and crinkly as you do this.

Repeat steps 1 through 3 until you have several of these twisted paper cases.

4 BUNCH

Glue or tape the twisted bases together. A bunch of eight creates a nice, full flower.

5 EXPERIMENT

Try making multicoloured flowers and using different-sized paper cases!

Fabbo flower jacket

I made my first floral jacket using a bunch of leftover fake flowers from my birthday party, and I can tell you now ... there is nothing quite like it! I find fake flowers that have a flat base, or a little plastic backing on them, are the best for this project.

YOU WILL NEED

· 1 old jacket (fake fur adds a nice volume to the design)

· hot glue gun

· at least 100 fake flowers, plastic stems removed

HOW TO: FABBO FLOWER JACKET

1.

....

Dab some glue on the backs of
your flowers and start gluing
them onto your jacket. I find
that gluing in sections is
best, starting at the shoulders
and working your way down until
the jacket is covered. Don't
feel like you have to go crazy
applying flowers underneath the
sleeves and in the armpit area.
As long as everywhere else is
covered, you won't even notice!

2.

....

As you go, glue some petals
together to make the design
look extra lush (and as
though the flowers are truly
connected).

Bouquet headphones

To me, headphones have always been an obvious opportunity for glorifying! Here is my simple take on livening up your old (or new) pair. Plug into your favourite music and enjoy feeling like a human bouquet!

YOU WILL NEED

· 1 pair of headphones

· hot glue gun

· about 40 small fake flowers, stems removed

· 10-15 fake green leaves and sprigs

· 20-30 fake pearls and gems

HOW TO: BOUQUET HEADPHONES

1.

Dab some glue on the backs of a few flowers and affix them to the top of your headphones. Work your way down each side until you have covered the whole pair. Don't be afraid to overlap them!

2.

Glue the green sprigs and leaves into the arrangement. They're great for filling any gaps in the design.

3.

For added dazzle, glue on some pearls and gems. Keep adding them to the petals and the actual headphones until you are happy with how it looks.

Blossoming jeans

Who doesn't have an old pair of neglected jeans stuffed at the back of the cupboard just waiting to BLOSSOM?

YOU WILL NEED

· 1 pair of old jeans

· hot glue gun

· about 60 medium fake
  flowers, stems removed

· about 50 sequins

· about 100 gems in a variety
  of colours and sizes

HOW TO: BLOSSOMING JEANS

1.

Starting at one knee, glue
some flowers onto your jeans.
Cluster them quite close
together to start, but let
them spread out a bit as you
work your way up and down the
leg. I like to place a few
stray flowers at the waistband
and cuffs to make it appear
as though the flowers are
cascading down the legs.

2.

Glue some sequins and gems
to the flowers' petals, then
extend this embellishment onto
the denim. I leave no more
than a 1 cm (½ in) gap between
my embellishments, as I find
this makes the design look
extra lush!

Bloomin' gorgeous paper rosette

If you don't want to wear your heart on your sleeve, consider wearing your feelings on your jacket!

YOU WILL NEED

- four 10 x 20 cm (4 x 8 in) strips of orange card
- 10 cm (4 in) scalloped circle punch or scissors
- 1 sheet of pink card
- hot glue gun
- felt pen
- a handful of small fake flower buds, stems removed
- 12 small sequins
- 5 small gems
- 3 fake pearls
- 1 badge back
- scissors
- 4 x 15 cm (1½ x 6 in) strip of blue card

HOW TO: BLOOMIN' GORGEOUS PAPER ROSETTE

1.
....

Fold one of your orange card strips in half, then fold it back and forth to create what looks like an accordion. Repeat this process with the other three strips.

2.
....

Glue your accordions together to make a circle. This will form the foundation of your rosette.

3.
....

Fold the pink card in half. Using your circle punch, cut two circles out of the pink card. If you don't have a circle punch, you can just use scissors. Use the felt pen to write whatever you want on the front circle.

4.
....

Place a line of glue along the circles' edges and fix them to the front and back of the accordion, creating something along the lines of an ice-cream sandwich.

5.
....

Glue the flowers around the front circle, tucking them among the accordion's folds.

6.
....

Glue your sequins, gems and pearls onto the front in whatever way you fancy. I like to place the pearls and gems at random points among the flowers and the sequins on the orange part of the rosette.

7.
....

Glue the badge back onto the back of the rosette.

8.
....

Snip a triangle out of one end of your blue strip of card. Glue the other end to the back of the rosette below the badge back, making sure the triangle end is hanging down and visible.

Floral petite party hat

A perfect cake or table topper and a wonderful garnish for any hairdo, this mini party hat will brighten up all festive affairs!

YOU WILL NEED

· 1 sheet of coloured card

· stapler

· hot glue gun

· 3 pipe cleaners

· scissors

· a smattering of small gems

· 6 small fake flowers, stems removed

· 1 hair comb (optional)

HOW TO: FLORAL PETITE PARTY HAT

1.

Take one corner of your piece of card and fold it over to make a cone shape. Staple the overlapping edges of your cone together. At this point, your cone will be quite long, so trim off the excess so that your party hat is the height you are after. The party hat shown on page 101 is 13 cm (5 in) tall.

2.

Squeeze a line of glue onto the wide bottom edge of your cone and attach a length of pipe cleaner - it'll give your hat a lovely finished trim! Continue gluing pipe cleaners around the cone in strips, leaving approximately 5 cm (2 in) between each. Trim off any excess.

3.

Glue the gems in a random pattern all over the hat.

4.

Glue some flowers to the pointed top of the hat and to one side of the party hat's base.

5.

If you want to wear your petite party hat, squeeze a blob of glue onto your hair comb and press it to the edge of your party hat. This will allow it to slide into your hair with ease.

Patty cake flower crown

This is the perfect project to show off your paper (cupcake) case blooms and create a unique garnish for any ensemble!

YOU WILL NEED

....

- about 25 yellow handmade flowers (pages 86-7)
- about 25 pink handmade flowers (pages 86-7)
- 1 plastic or fabric headband, at least 3 cm (1¼ in) wide
- hot glue gun
- some fake gems and pearls (optional)

HOW TO: PATTY CAKE FLOWER CROWN

1.

Glue your flowers onto the headband, leaving 5 cm (2 in) bare at each end so it will sit easily behind your ears.

2.

Once you've covered your headband, start building up the design by gluing flowers on top of one another. You want them to appear like bunches as you layer them, so really go for it - make the design compact.

3.

If you want, embellish your crown by gluing on some gems and pearls.

Bloom-and-sparkle dress

This project merges two of my favourite things: flowers and gems!

YOU WILL NEED

- 1 old solid-coloured dress (a lighter colour helps your embellishments really pop)

- hot glue gun

- 200 each of gems, beads, pearls, buttons, sequins and other shiny bits

- about 50 fake flowers, stems removed

HOW TO: BLOOM-AND-SPARKLE DRESS

1.

Set aside half a day (or maybe enlist some willing friends) to glue a mass of lovely gems, beads, sequins and other sparkly bits onto your dress. Implement the mosaic tip (page 9) here: you want to evenly space out your gems and other embellishments.

2.

Once your dress is completely encrusted, glue a smattering of flowers onto the shoulders, bust and sleeves. I like to glue a few on the waist and skirt, too, as though the blooms have just naturally sprouted there. The whole thing will dry in seconds and be ready to wear!

Thank you

Big thanks to my husband Thomas for his unwavering support, assistance and photo-taking help while putting this book together. Also, love and thanks to my family and friends, who provide a happy break from a self-induced craft haze. Thanks must also be given to my two poochies, Daphne and Daisy, who are always ready with well-timed barks and hugs.

About Rachel Burke

Rachel Burke is a multidisciplinary artist based in Brisbane, Australia. Working as a designer for her namesake label and as a freelance creative, Rachel has created works for clients including Etsy, *frankie* magazine, Queensland Art Gallery | Gallery of Modern Art, UNIQLO, and Splendour in the Grass Music and Arts Festival. She is also the author of *Daphne and Daisy: Pawtraits of Sausage Style*.

BE NICE TO
YOURSELF &
DON'T BE A
DRAGON TO LIVE
WITH ☺♡☺

Contents

Listening summary – page 42

Speaking summary – page 53

Tips for IELTS Skills Checklists - page 62–64

Sam McCarter

Tips for
IELTS

A must-have for all IELTS candidates!

MACMILLAN

Macmillan Education
Between Towns Road, Oxford OX4 3PP
A division of Macmillan Publishers Limited
Companies and representatives throughout the world

ISBN : 978-1-4050-9616-4

Text © Sam McCarter 2006
Design and illustration © Macmillan Publishers Limited 2006
First published 2006

Note to students and teachers

Photocopies may be made for classroom use of pages 62–64 without
the prior permission of Macmillan Publishers Limited. However, please
note that the copyright law, which does not normally permit multiple
copying of published material, applies to the rest of this book.

Designed by eMC Design

Cover design by Andrew Oliver

The author and the publisher would like to thank Liz Hunt, Roger
Townsend, Paula Nelson and Susan Hutchison for their help and
contribution.

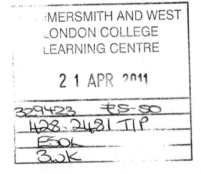
Printed in Thailand

2013 2012 2011 2010
10 9 8 7 6 5 4

Reading

Exam summary

- The academic reading module takes 60 minutes.
- There are three reading texts with a total of 1500–2500 words.
  - The texts can be on a range of different topics.
  - At least one of the texts will contain a detailed logical argument.
  - The texts become progressively more difficult to understand.
- There are usually 40 questions. These questions become progressively more difficult.
- The reading component is weighted. The standard is the same on each test day. However, to reach a specific band, the number of correct answers required is different in each exam.

Golden rules

- Answer the questions quickly and accurately. If you can't do a question quickly, leave it and come back to it later.
- As the passages are long, you don't have to read them in detail. Skim and scan them to find the relevant information.
- The level, the texts and the tasks become progressively more difficult. Therefore, do the earlier questions as quickly as possible, to give yourself more time for the difficult questions.
- You have roughly one and a half minutes for each question.
- Do not panic if you can only do maybe three questions out of seven. Go through them again and again, but quickly.
- When you finish one passage, check your answers and try to fill any gaps.
- The questions generally follow the order of the information in the text. However, the questions in one section can overlap another and they may be jumbled.
- The questions are usually paraphrases of the text so look for the meaning in the text, not the exact words.

- The questions test general understanding [G] and specific detail [S]:
  - Matching headings [G]
  - Multiple-choice questions [G and S]
  - Summary/flow-chart/table completion [G and S]
  - Classification [G and S]
  - Matching sentences from a suitable list [G and S]
  - Answering *Yes, No, Not Given* [G and S]
  - Answering *True, False, Not Given* [G and S]
  - Matching stems to sentences endings [S]
  - Sentence completion [S]
  - Short answer questions [S]

- Some question types are used to see how you deal with specific information and general meaning. For example, a multiple-choice question can test for detail or understanding of a whole text.

- The questions do not test your *knowledge* of English, but your ability to *use* your English. The exam is testing whether you can use your English to find your way around a written English text.

Techniques to increase your speed

Learn to use the following techniques separately, to switch automatically and to use several at one time:

- *Skimming*. Skim the text to obtain general information. Think about the general information and not the detail. Don't underline.

- *Scanning*. Scan for specific detail only; don't concentrate on the meaning of the text. If you start to read, or even to skim, you will find it more difficult to locate your words.

- *Skim and read*. Skim a text, and stop at particular points to look at the meaning. Use the questions to guide you around the text.

- *Scan and skim*. When you scan a text for a specific word, your eye touches the other information lightly. Because your focus is on the scanning, your eye skims the text naturally and does not slow you down. You need to practice to build your confidence.

Skimming

Basic skimming techniques

Skim the title and the questions. They give you a summary of the passage.

Skim the content words only, i.e. the *nouns, main verbs, adjectives* and *adverbs*. Do not look at words like *the, a, in, is,* etc. Underline the content words in a few paragraphs. Then read them again.

Skim only the basic structure of the sentences/clauses: the *subject, verb,* and the *object* (if there is one). Don't look at adverbs and adjectives.

Without reading the text, mark the connecting words, e.g. *moreover, in addition, however,* etc. Practise until you can see the connecting words automatically when you look at a paragraph. Then you do not need to mark them.

Skim so that you recognize common types of paragraph organization, like *effects, causes, methods, etc.* See *Matching headings to paragraphs on page 12.*

Skim only the nouns in the text to give you a general picture. Be clear about the differences between: a noun, verb adjective and adverb. Learn to recognize them and know what their function is in the sentence.

Intermediate skimming techniques

7 Read the first sentence of a paragraph and then skim the beginning of each sentence in the paragraph. This will show you the general theme of the paragraph. ➤➤ See *Text organization* below. For example:

His career was rather chequered, spanning a period of 30 years. He ... After resigning, he ... Not long after he ... Van Damme then ....

The referring word *he* carries the information through the subsequent sentences.

8 Ignore and do not underline words you do not know. Focusing on words you do not know will slow you down.

9 Skim the verbs in each sentence. This shows you if the content of the text is changing.

10 Start at the verb in each sentence and look at everything after that. The verb usually marks the beginning of new information in the sentence.

11 Cover the left hand or right hand side of a text and skim. This stops you concentrating too hard on the meaning.

12 Skim a text to understand a theme. This can be factual or ideas. For example, skim a text *line by line* without looking at the meaning and pick out words that form a pattern/ picture or that have something in common. As you skim, remember writers have to avoid repetition so they have to use synonyms to create a theme.

Advanced skimming techniques

13 Skim the text forwards or backwards and note words which form a general picture: *airports, passengers, lounge, fly.*

14 Locate the focus of the paragraph. It is not always at the beginning. ►► See *Writing* page 35 for words like *problems, ideas* that help you.

15 Use your own knowledge of different types of sentences and paragraph organzations to predict and move around the passage. ►► See *Writing, How to organize a paragraph* page 35.

16 Look at a central point in a paragraph and then allow your eye to wander around the paragraph skimming the nouns, verbs for the general idea.

17 Use the questions to help you navigate text. ►► See *Writing, Analysing the essay questions and understanding the rubric* on page 33.

Seven skimming tricks

1 Use a pencil to help you skim. This helps train your eye.

2 Skim each sentence from left to right.

3 When you develop confidence, skim left to right and then right to left and so on.

4 Move a pencil vertically down through the centre of the text forcing your eye to look quickly at the text on either side.

5 Skim diagonally through the text – top left to bottom right. You could also go backwards diagonally or vertically.

6 Jump in different directions through the text. Then stop now and again and read.

7 Skim the ends of sentences. A sentence is basically divided between information which refers back to the previous sentence and information which is new. Information which refers generally comes at the beginning and new ideas at the end. Skim the end of the sentences. Example: *A man walked into a shop. The man picked up a newspaper. The newspaper ...*

At all times try not to get caught up in the detail.

Scanning

Choosing scanning words in the questions

Choose your scanning words carefully. For example, with *True*, *False*, *Not Given*, read all the statements and look for words that occur frequently. These are likely to be the general subject of the passage, so they will not help you scan.

Look for words that relate to the general subject. They can be nouns, names, dates, etc.

Keep in mind the basic structure of a sentence: *Subject, Verb, Object*. Anything extra qualifies the sentence, e.g. additional clauses, adjectives, adverbs, negative words, comparisons. These words/phrases help you understand the focus of the statement. For example, you should notice a negative word like *ignore* immediately. It is probably not a scanning word, but a word that tests your understanding of the text.

Look for words and ideas that help you navigate the text. *This is a very efficient tool.* Look at the questions together and not in isolation. The questions can often be subdivided: two relating to one area of text; three to another, etc. Connect the questions, group them and use this to help you to jump around the text.

How to scan slowly

Scan from left to right, left to right. You must look only for your chosen scanning words. If you do not, this will be a slow and ineffective technique.

~~Text Text Text Text Text Text~~
~~Text Text Text Text Text Text~~

How to scan quickly

To stop yourself from reading every word, start at the end of each line or paragraph. Scan from right to left, right to left backwards through the text. This prevents you from reading the text.

~~Text Text Text Text Text Text~~
~~Text Text Text Text Text Text~~

Alternatively, scan diagonally through the text from bottom right to top left, or vertically, from the bottom to the top.

Text Text Text Text Text Text
Text Text Text Text Text Text
Text Text Text Text Text Text

- Move through the text in a zigzag backwards. This stops you from reading. Move faster each time you practise.

Text Text Text Text Text Text
Text Text Text Text Text Text

You can also scan forward, but you must stop yourself reading the text.

Text Text Text Text Text Text
Text Text Text Text Text Text

- When you have gained confidence, scan forwards left to right, right to left and so on. You do not have to waste time going to the beginning of a line each time!

Text Text Text Text Text Text
Text Text Text Text Text Text

- Very efficient readers can look at the centre of a paragraph and do not allow their eye to move. They then take everything in around the central point. If a paragraph is long, do it in stages.

Text Text Text Text Text Text
Text Text Text Text Text Text
Text Text Tex●Text Text Text
Text Text Text Text Text Text
Text Text Text Text Text Text

You will pick up meaning as you scan. You are then becoming an efficient reader!

ow to mark the text when you skim or scan

Use a pencil so you can rub out mistakes.

Only underline key words: scanning words from the questions and organizing words.

Underline as little as possible. Too much underlining makes it difficult to find essential information. Remember more is less.

Compare:

> The underlined effects of lack of investment can be seen clearly in the state of the trains and the stations. The carriages are old-fashioned and generally in a bad state of repair, factors which put people off using public transport. People are often frightened to travel at night because there are no guards on the trains and the stations deserted...

> The effects of lack of investment can be seen clearly in the state of the trains and the stations. The carriages are old-fashioned and generally in a bad state of repair, factors which put people off using public transport. People are often frightened to travel at night because there are no guards on the trains and the stations deserted...

Develop a simple underlining code. Use a box ☐ for focus words like *measures*, etc. Underline main ideas. Use a zigzag line ⋀⋁ for detail.

If you are fast, use this code in the exam. If not, just underline. It helps you focus on the organization of the text.

ompleting the answer sheet

Fill in the answer sheet carefully. Use a pencil.

Mark the end of the first two passages on the sheet with a short line. Aim to complete one stage at a time.

Fill in the answers directly onto the sheet and in the correct order.

Write clearly. Give only one answer unless the instructions require more.

Write in the correct spaces and keep within them.

Check your spelling, especially common words and follow the word limit.

Do not copy words from the question stem or paraphrases from the text. The answer will be marked incorrect.

Skim/check your answers when you finish. Choose answers at random to check, or check them backwards. Also check your answers against the questions to make sure the grammar is correct.

Matching headings to paragraphs

- Matching headings with paragraphs tests your ability to understand general information.

- Look always for the most general heading. This may be the first paragraph or the conclusion.

- Always do exercises with headings first, as the headings summarize the text. They help you scan the answers to the other questions.

- Look at any titles with the passage.

- Look at the example, if there is one. Don't just cross it out. It may be the introduction, which organizes the other headings.

- The example may be of the second or another paragraph. Still use the heading to predict the headings next to it.

- If there are only a few paragraph headings to match there will probably not be an example.

- Read the instructions. Check if you can use a heading more than once.

- Sometimes there are more paragraphs than headings, so you need to skim quickly.

- If the list of headings is long, reveal them one at a time to stop panicking.

Technique 1: analyse the grammar and vocabulary in the headings

- Distinguish between the two types of words used: *information specific to the paragraph* and *organizing words*.

- Organizing words like plural countable words are common, e.g. *causes, reasons, advantages, drawbacks, difficulties, responses, problems, effects, solutions, factors, dangers, examples,* etc. Learn to recognize how these are expressed in a text. Be aware of similar words.

  Note that the specific information about the paragraph is added on to these organizing words: [causes] *of poverty in urban areas*; [different levels] *of urban poverty* Note how the phrases in italics narrow the meaning of the organizing words in brackets.

  Use this division of information to help you skim/scan paragraphs. Look for paragraphs that describe *effect, levels, problems,* etc. Then see if they contain the specific information in the rest of the heading.

- Plural organizing words indicate the paragraph has more than one idea or a list of ideas probably with an introduction.

- A paragraph can be organized around uncountable words: *damage,* etc. It can be organized around countable singular nouns where the paragraph is describing one item: *a comparison, impact, development,* etc.

echnique 2: search for connections between headings

Headings are usually connected with each other.

Check for a heading that looks specific; it could be a detail in a paragraph and therefore a distracter for a general heading. If you removed this detail from the paragraph, would it still remain intact?

A heading that looks specific could be a heading for paragraph describing just one detail.

Check for headings that relate to each other: *cause/effect; problem/solution.*

Check for headings with adjectives, which qualify nouns. Make sure the heading covers all aspects of the paragraph. Don't forget about the adjective or other qualifying phrases.

Headings can have two pieces of information where one is referring back to the previous paragraph.

Advanced techniques

Read the headings and skim a paragraph quickly. Make a decision quickly.

Expand the heading into a sentence. This might make the meaning clearer.

When you find the general theme or focus of the paragraph, stop skimming and match quickly.

Once you have matched the headings, read them in order and see if the sequence makes sense.

When you check, avoid looking at the detail, as it can make you change your mind.

Predict a possible sequence of headings before you look at the text.

If a paragraph is difficult, use the various skimming techniques focusing on text development. Always look for change of direction in a text.

Skim each paragraph in turn and then decide very quickly what it is about. Make your own heading in a couple of words. Then look at the list of headings and match.

Matching sentences/phrases to paragraphs

- ➤➤ See *Matching headings to paragraphs* on page 12 and follow the same basic techniques.

- As there are usually more paragraphs than sentences/phrases, you need to scan quickly

- The sentences can relate to specific detail in a text. Look for general nouns, which summarize, like *description, references, cause, effect, importance,* etc. The words can be both singular and plural.

- As well as phrases linked to a general noun, there may be clauses introduced by *how* or statements of fact: *the fact that ....*

- Plural words are likely to indicate that the phrase/sentence covers a whole paragraph, so it is like a heading. A singular noun can also cover a whole or a part of a paragraph.

- If the phrases look like headings or lists, then look for a series of points.

  Use the technique of skimming/scanning a paragraph for the organization as described in Technique 1 on Page 12.

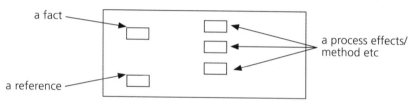

- When you have found the information, check that the focus of the phrase paraphrases summarizes the text.

Completing summaries with and without a wordlist

Stage 1

- Check the instructions to find the word limit. It is usually one/two or three words – always keep this in mind.

- Also check if you can use a word/phrase more than once.

- Skim the summary first to get an idea of the overall meaning.

- Work out the grammar needed to fill in each space.

- When you are working out the answers, say the word *blank* for the space. Don't jump across to the word on the other side of the blank. For example, if you read *Candidates need to pay _____ to detail,* it is more difficult to feel what the missing word is. If you read *Candidates need to pay blank to detail,* it is easier to predict the missing word.

tage 2

Use collocation of words and ideas where possible to predict the answer and then check the text.

Try to predict the answer by giving your own word. It is easier to match your own word than an empty space.

Predict using general words. For example, you may know that the blank is a person. Look for this in the passage.

The more aware you are of the general idea of the text, the closer your answer will be.

If you are asked to complete with up to three words, try to think of a general word.

tage 3

Look at the text and match your words with words in the passage.

Be careful with any changes in the grammatical form of a word.

Skim the summary again with your words in place to check the overall meaning and then, if you have time, skim the text.

When you put the answers in the Answer Sheet check the spelling is correct.

If you have a wordlist, note the words/phrases in the list will usually have letters attached, A, B, C, etc. So you will only have to write a letter in the Answer Sheet.

Read the list and insert the words/phrases one at a time, isolating the relevant grammar. This helps you see if the items are correct and fill the other blanks.

nswering multiple-choice questions

In some cases, there may be five alternatives (A–E) rather than four. If there are five alternatives, you may have to choose one or more answers.

Multiple-choice questions are like *True*, *False*, *Not Given* questions. One of the alternatives creates a statement, which is *True*. The other three are either contradictions or *Not Given*.

Multiple-choice questions test specific detail where you are asked to analyse one part of a text, e.g. a fact.

A multiple-choice question can test your understanding of the whole text, e.g. a question at the end about the purpose of the passage or with possible titles or summaries.

Stage 1

- Skim read all the questions for the passage to get the general picture.

- As you practise, and in the exam itself, cover the alternatives (A–D) with a pencil or a piece of paper and read the stem only.

- Focus on content words like nouns, names, verbs, etc. and also words that qualify the part of the sentence. Distinguish between the general topic of the passage and specific scanning words.

- Words that help qualify the stem help you to match it with an alternative and vice versa. So look for words like *more*, *usually*, modals like *should*, etc. and words that add qualities.

- Predict the answer where you can and try to complete the stem yourself. If the stem contains a cause, then you probably want an effect at the end of the sentence.
  ➤➤ See *Reading* page 20 for general tips about prediction in reading.

- Reveal the first alternative and think about it quickly. Again focus on content and qualifying words.

- Read the stem again and reveal each of the alternatives in turn. It is easy to forget about the stem by the time you get to alternative D!

- Underline words that will help you as you scan.

Stage 2

- Group the alternatives. Look for information that the alternatives have in common or that is different.

  - The alternatives may all be variations of the same basic detail with one piece of information that is different.

  - There may be two alternatives that are similar and two that are very different.

  - There may be two alternatives that contradict each other.

- Remember that if alternatives are the same, neither can be the answer.

- Keeping in mind the general picture of the passage, read the alternatives and predict the answer. Scan the passage to locate the answer and check your prediction.

- To prevent panic, think about the question and the text separately.

- When you are checking your prediction with the text, read the relevant part of the text and look away from the page when you are thinking.

Other strategies

- When you predict the answer by matching the stem with an alternative, think about which information logically fits together. Keep in mind the logic of the other questions and the passage.

- Read the answers to the multiple-choice questions you have done. Check that they form a logical picture.

- Do not answer the questions in isolation from each other.

A variation of the standard multiple-choice question is where you chose two items mentioned by the writer from a list of five. The same techniques apply.

Completing sentences

- Sentence completion exercises test your ability to extract specific detail from a text.

- Skim all the questions in the section.

- Work out what information is being tested.

- Check the word limit in the instructions.

- Read the stem of the sentence for completion and try to understand the meaning.

- Note any words that help you scan the text for the answer.

- Decide the grammar that you need to finish the sentence; most of the time it is a noun/ noun phrase.

- Predict whether the answer contains an adjective only; an adjective and a noun; a gerund and a noun; or a gerund, an adjective and a noun.

- Try to look for more than one answer at the same time.

Answering questions

- ➤➤ See *Completing sentences* above and *Completing tables, flowcharts and diagrams* on page 18 and follow the same procedures.

- Look at the grammar of the question.

- Check what the question word at the beginning is. *What/Which/Who/Where* need nouns as answers. The word *How* may need: *by + -ing*, etc. or an adverb.

Completing tables, flowcharts and diagrams

- ➤➤ See *Completing sentences* on page 17 and follow the same procedures.

- Make sure you skim the whole flowchart to get the overall meaning.

- Tables are often quite long. Don't panic – remember, if a set of questions looks long, it is usually because it is easy.

- Check the grammar of the table/flowchart/diagram, i.e. is it in note form?

- The chart is usually in columns with headings. Check the types of words of the other items in each column.

- If you have a wordlist, follow the same procedure as for summaries. With diagrams find a reference point and work slowly round the diagram.

Matching names/dates to ideas

- You may be asked to match:

  - catagories, names or dates with statements which are paraphrases of the text.

  - sentences which are paraphrases of particular items in a list.

  In all cases, the basic techniques are the same.

- ➤➤ See *Matching sentences/phrases to paragraphs* on page 14 and follow the same procedures.

- Check if any name, catagory, etc. matches with more than one item.

- Read the names etc. and the statements.

- Note anything you are already aware of from reading the other questions.

- Read *all* the statements rather than just one at a time. You may then be able to match more than one at a time.

- If the list is long, reveal each item one at a time using your pencil to help you focus.

- Scan the passage for the names etc. Mark all of them first. Put a box around them to make it easier to distinguish between the names etc. and other underlined words.

- If you cannot find one name etc., quickly go on to the next. You may find the one you have missed while you are looking for something else.

- When you have finished, check you have entered your answers correctly and skim check the answers in the names and answers in the text.

- Make sure you do not contradict the other answers you have made.

Matching stems to sentences

• Skim the instructions, the sentence stems and the ends of sentences.

• Read through the stems to understand the meaning and underline only essential words.

• Try to predict which ending matches the stem. To help you, reveal them one at a time.

• Even if you cannot predict any of the answers, practise the technique of prediction. With practice, you will be able to see that ideas, like words in phrases/collocations, fit together. Knowing this will help you.

• If you have difficulty dealing with the information, break up the ideas and see if each part matches. Always think about meaning rather than words.

Matching questions to sentences

• ➤➤ See *Matching stems to sentences* above and follow the same procedures.

• If the list of alternatives to choose from is long, reveal them one at a time.

Answering *True, False, Not Given* questions

• In *True/False* exercises, *False* covers *False* and *Not Given*. If a statement is not *True* according to the text, it is classed as *False*. The statement can be *False*

  – because it contradicts the information in some way.

  – because there is no information about the statement in the passage.

  These two aspects of *False* can then become separate items *False* and *Not Given*.

• A *False* statement contradicts the information in a passage:

  – because it is the direct opposite of the original text, e.g. the text says *North*, but the statement says *South*.

  – because it is the negative of the meaning in the original text.

  – because it is neither of these, but it is not the same as the information in the text.

Technique 1: analysing the statements

- If you read the statements in sequence, you can sometimes see where the information moves from relating to one paragraph to the next paragraph. Practise reading this type of statement without the text to see the development.

- Turn the statement into a question. You then have to answer *Yes/No*. If you can't, the answer is *Not Given*.

- Find the central or focal point of the statement. Imagine you are reading the statement aloud – where is the likely stress in the sentence?

- Look for words that qualify the sentence or make the sentence restrictive like *only, little, not many, sometimes, usually, largely,* etc. or agents like *by the police,* etc. or impersonal phrases like *it is suggested*.

- Look for words that are negative, e.g. *ignore, refuse, deny, reject* or words that are positive like *cover, help, like, favour,* etc.

- Look for comparisons of any kind.

- Check for further/previous plans/projects/ideas, etc. Maybe no information is given about 'others'.

- Reveal the statements one at a time to help you focus on them.

Technique 2: predicting and checking

- When you are thinking about the statement, use common sense to predict the answer. Check your prediction in the text.

- Understand the statement *before* you look at the text. Don't just underline the words that help you to scan for the answer in the text.

- When you find the information, analyse the text without thinking about the statement. This will stop you getting confused. Then read the statement carefully, look at the text and decide.

- When you are making your decision, follow the process of reading the statement, then the text.

- If you read the statement, the text and then the statement again, you may get the wrong answer. For example:

Text: *The price will fall soon*.

Statement: *The price will go down*.

Answer: *True*.

Compare this with the following:

Text: *The price will go down*.

Statement: *The price will fall soon*.

Answer: *Not Given*.

- When you have finished, read the statements again in sequence and see if your answers fit the overall picture you have of the passage.

Answering *Yes, No, Not Given* questions

- The principles are the same as for *True, False, Not Given*. This type of question is used to analyse the claims or opinions of a writer.

- You need to make sure that the opinions that are given are those of the writer and not opinions of others reported by the writer.

- Questions can contain statements which pass a judgement on or evaluate a situation which is described in the text.

- Always check for comparisons. Comparisons are simple ways to make a comment and pass judgement. For example, in the statement *Swimming is more relaxing than walking,* a judgment is being made about the two items because one is put above the other.

- Always check for any adjective that judges a situation, e.g. *sensible, difficult demanding*. Any adjective can pass a judgement, even simple adjectives like *big*: *That building is big*. Another person may not agree!

- Check always for adverbs in the question like *never, always, frequently, carefully,* etc as they will also change the meaning of a basic statement.

- Check for questions which contain reasons: *because, as, since,* etc.

- Check for any mention of development progression change … *increasing/increasingly/rapidly … is improving* … Ask yourself if change is taking place.

- Check for contrast with numbers, e.g. *a solution* in the question as opposed to *a range of solutions* in the text. Distinguish between general and specific.

Writing

Exam summary

- The academic writing module takes approximately 60 minutes.

- There are two tasks.

Task 1

- This takes about 20 minutes. You write a report about a graph, table, bar chart or diagram, using a minimum of 150 words.

- You are marked on task completion and use of a range of vocabulary and grammar, organization and development.

Task 2

- This takes about 40 minutes. You write an essay discussing an argument, opinion or a point of view.

- You may be asked to write about one or more specific aspects of a topic: *causes, effects, solutions, factors, problems, measures, steps, proposals, recommendations, suggestions, arguments of other people for/against, reasons, dangers, advantages and/or disadvantages,* etc.

- You may be asked to give your opinion and suggestions for causes and solutions.

- You are marked on use of a range of vocabulary and grammar, organization and development and how you respond to the task. Specialist knowledge of the subject is not being tested.

Task 1

Golden rules

- Do Task 1 first. There is a reason why it is Task 1! From the psychological point of view, it gives you a sense of accomplishment when you have finished it.

- A common feature of the writing process is the concept of getting oneself going. With the shorter Task you can get yourself into your stride in writing. By the time you start Task 2, you will then be much more alert and perform Task 2 much more efficiently.

- Spend 20 minutes on this task. A common mistake which candidates make is to spend longer on Task 2 and leave themselves 15 minutes or less to complete Task 1.

- Take Task 1 seriously, even though Task 2 carries double the marks.

- Skim the instructions and study the diagram. Use the general statement about the data to help you interpret the graph.

- Spend the recommended 20 minutes as follows:

  - 2–3 minutes analysing and planning

  - 14–15 minutes writing

  - 2–3 minutes checking

- Check the values and numbers on the vertical and horizontal axes.

- Work out how many lines 150 words are in your handwriting, e.g. if you write about 10 words per line, then you will need to produce at least 15 lines. Aim to write no more than 170/180 words.

- Check that you have written *at least* 150 words. If you write less, it will affect your score.

- Compare general trends, differences, etc and support this with information from the diagram. Avoid focusing too closely on the details.

- If you have more than one graph or chart or mixture, link the information.

- Make sure you write in paragraphs: an introduction, one or two paragraphs for the body of the text. Then write a brief conclusion.

Graphs

How to write the introduction

- One sentence is enough for the introduction.

- Replace words in the general statement with synonyms or paraphrases where you can.

- If you cannot quickly write your introduction in your own words, do not waste time. Write out the words in the rubric, but remember to change them later.

- Do not write the word *below* from the rubric in your introduction.

- Use one of the following four prompts to help you write an introduction:

  - *The graph shows/illustrates the trends in ... between ... and ...*

  - *The graph gives/provides/reveals/presents information about (the differences/ changes ...)*

  - *The graph shows that (there is a number of differences between ...)*

  - *The graph shows/illustrates how the sales have differed/changed ...*

- Vary noun phrases, e.g. *sales/purchases of different cars; sales/purchases of private vehicles; the number of various types of cars sold/purchased; the number of various types of cars sold/purchased; car sales/purchases.*

- Use general words for the introduction: *information, data, difference(s), similarities, changes, trends, results, numbers, percentages, figures, statistics, breakdown.*

How to write the main part of the text

- Divide your text into 3–4 paragraphs, including the introduction.

- Divide the information into *broad/general groups/categories* or *trends.*

- Describe the *main* or *most striking/significant/noticeable/outstanding/remarkable feature(s)/characteristics differences/trends/changes.* Avoid writing lists of detail. Write about general trends and support what you say with specific data.

- Describe the three general trends: *is/was upwards/downwards/flat* or say what happened: *...(sales) rose/fell/remained flat/fluctuated ...*

Use appropriate synonyms:

- **rise** (vb): *climb, go up, increase, improve, jump, leap, move upward, rocket, skyrocket, soar, shoot up, pick up, surge, recover*

- **rise** (n): *increase, climb, jump, leap, pick up, surge (in)*

- **fall** (vb): *collapse, decline, decrease, deteriorate, dip, dive, drop, fall (back), go down, go into free-fall, plummet, plunge, reduce* (only in the passive) *slide, slip (back), slump, take a nosedive*

- **fall** (n): *decline, decrease, deterioration, dip, drop, plunge, free-fall, slide, slip, dive, reduction, slump*

- **fluctuate**: (noun: *fluctuations*) *be erratic, be fitful, vary, rise and fall erratically*

- **flat**: *no change, constant*

Add suitable adverbs: *dramatically, erratically, gradually, markedly, significantly, slightly, slowly, steadily.*

Add specific information or examples:

- *(increasing* etc.*) from … to …*

- *between … and …*

- *with an increase from … to … /to … from …*

Use: *…followed by …* to add more information.

Add time phrases:

- *between … and …*

- *from … to … (inclusive)*

- *at …/by …/in …*

- *in the year (1994) …*

- *during/over the period … to …*

- *over the latter half of the year/century/decade/period*

- *over the next past/previous five days/weeks/months/years/decades*

How to compare and contrast

- Repeat the process for each general point, but vary the sentence structure, grammar and vocabulary.

- ➤➤ See *Bar charts* on page 27 and use the comparing and contrasting language give there: ... *increased more than; there was a greater increase in ... than ...*

- Use conjunctions like: *while/whilst/whereas/but*

- Use linkers: *however/in contrast/by comparison/meanwhile/on the other hand*

- Focus on an item in the graph:

  - As regards (sales), they ...

  - *With regard to/Regarding/In the case of/As for/Turning to (sales), they ...*

  - *Where _____ is/are concerned/it/they ...*

  - *When it comes to _____, it/they ...*

- Use these words and phrases to describe predictions:

  - *It is predicted/forecast(ed)/estimated/expected/projected anticipated that ... will ...*

  - *... will ...*

  - *... will have ... by ...*

  - *The projection is for ... to ...*

  - *... is/are predicted/forecast(ed)/estimated/expected/projected/ anticipated to*

  - *... is/are set to*

- Use the present perfect to describe the recent past to the present: ...*has risen*, etc.

- Write a conclusion. One sentence is enough. You can use the following phrases: *Generally, ...; Generally speaking, ...; All in all, ...; On average, ...; Overall, ...; It is clear/evident/obvious that, ...*

Other verb sequences stages you can use:

- ... rose from ... to ...

- ... *rose ... and increased ... from ... to ...*

- ... *rose ..., increasing from ... to ...*

- ... *rose ..., overtaking ... in ..., and outstripping ... in ...*

- *Rising from ... to... (sales) overtook ... and outstripped ...*

- ... rose ... overtaking ... in ..., and reaching a peak ... in ...

- ... *rose ..., before leveling off ...*

- ... *fell ..., before rising ...*

- ... *fell ..., after rising.../after rising ..., ... fell ...*

- ... *rose/fell ... from ... to ..., while/whilst/whereas/ ... rose/fell ...*

ote how versatile the use of the gerund is. You can use it to explain; as part of series of ʼents and as a result.

ʼar charts

For bar charts that present data like graphs over a period of time, ➤➤ see *Graphs* on page 24.

The survey took place in the past not the present, but you can use either the past simple or the present simple to describe the data.

Try to classify the items and divide them into groups rather than writing about each one in turn: *the (factors) can be divided into two main groups ...*

- Name the groups: ... *namely those related to ... and those (connected) with ...*

- Compare the two groups: ... *of the two, the former is the larger.*

- State an important feature in this group: *with ... being the most popular with 40 per cent.*

- Compare and contrast the other items. Use some of the following:
  - *more/less than* …
  - *(bigger) than* …
  - *(not) as big as* …
  - *twice as big/much as* …
  - *rather than* …
  - *as against/as opposed to/compared with/in comparison with* …
  - *in (sharp) contrast to the biggest/smallest (change)* …
  - *more (women) cited/achieved/participated/took part in/were involved in* … *than* ..
  - *there were more (men) than (women) who* …
- To quote from the results of the survey, you can use:
  - … *percent quoted/cited/mentioned/considered* … *as important* …
  - … *was quoted/cited/mentioned/considered as the most/least important factor by*
  - … *came top/bottom/second/next, followed (closely) by* … *at* … *and* … *respectivel*

Pie charts

- Pie charts can be like bar charts except that various sections add up to 100%. There c also be a series of charts where the data show trends.
- There is often both a graph and a pie chart and the two are related.
- Make sure you show the connection between the pie and the graph or bar chart rath than just listing the data from the pie chart.
- Use the information regarding graphs to describe trends.
- If you have a graph and a pie chart, describe the graph, if it is the most important. Th link the information in the pie chart to the graph.
- Show that you are looking at the pie chart: *From the pie chart, it is clear/obvious/ evident that* …
- Relate a particular item in the pie chart to an aspect of the graph/chart: … *is related/ connected to/has an effect on/affects* … *, because* …
- You can compare/contrast items: … *while* …; *in contrast,* …
- You can use the pie chart to help you draw conclusions about the graph: *The pie char suggests that* … and show the relationship between the two.

▶▶ See *Graphs* and *Bar charts* on pages 24 and 27 and use this language to compare and contrast further, showing as many links as possible.

Always link data from different sources to each other.

ables

A table can contain data like pie charts, graphs and bar charts that are not related to a specific item in the past. Follow the steps described for these charts.

The presentation of information in tables can seem overwhelming. Don't panic! There is a simple way round this. If the table gives a lot of data over a number of years, at the end of the line draw a rough graph line to indicate the trend. Do this quickly for each item in the table. This means that you won't have to look at each number every time you want to analyse a line.

Because the numbers are given for each year, don't be tempted to include each individual piece of information.

Use general trends/statements, backed up by data as in the graphs. Sometimes highlight special changes/developments.

rocesses

Follow the same initial steps for writing about a graph.

In the introduction you can use: *The diagram/picture/chart shows/illustrates/describes/ depicts the process of/how …*

Find a starting point and write the process as a series of steps:

Useful connecting words you can use are:

− Adverbs: *first/firstly/first of all, secondly, thirdly, then/next/after that/following that/ following on from this/subsequently/subsequent to that, finally*

− Prepositions: *At the beginning of …; At the end of …*

Use the following conjunctions to make more complex sentences:

− *when/once/as soon as/immediately*

− *before* + clause or gerund

− *after* + clause or gerund

− *where/from where/after which*

- Other connecting devices you can use are:
    - *The first/next/final step/phase/stage is/involves* …
    - *After this step* …
    - *Once this stage is completed* …
    - *Following this* …
- In sequences, you can also use the gerund to show development.

Tenses and voice

- Use the present simple to describe processes.
- The agent is not usually mentioned unless a task is performed by a particular person.
- Use the passive voice if the process is describing something *being made*, like a book, e.g. *the book is printed and then collated, after which it is bound.*
- Use the active voice when you describe something which is happening: *The moisture evaporates and condenses on the* …
- Be very careful with singular and plural agreement in writing processes especially if you are using the active voice.
- When describing a cycle, you can conclude: The cycle *then repeats itself/is then repeated.*

Maps

- Follow the initial steps for analysing graphs and processes.
- If you are describing changes over a number of years, check the key carefully.
- Familiarize yourself with words showing location on the points of the compass: … *was constructed in the north/northwest; constructed north/northwest of the city/to the north/northwest of the city,* etc.
- Be careful with time phrases and tenses. With *in*, use the past simple passive:

  The stadium was constructed in the year 2000.

  With *by*, use the past perfect passive: *The stadium had been constructed by the year 2000.*

- Try to vary the structure of your sentences by putting the time phrase at the beginning and the end of the sentence. The same applies to the locations.

Some useful words and expressions:

- *in the centre of/next to/adjacent to*
- *built/erected/replaced*
- *situated/located*
- *changed into/added/gave way to/became/made way for/converted*
- *saw/witnessed considerable changes/developments*

Use adverbs like *moreover/in addition* etc. ➤➤ See *Task 2* on page 39.

The use of *while* is common: *while in 1995 …, by the year 2005 …*

aps where you have to choose between proposed locations

You are asked to choose which is the best location for a sports complex, etc.

Describe where: *It is proposed that the new … will be built …*

Explain why this site is more suitable than one or the other.

Describe the amenities which are nearby: *…because it will be next to/convenient for/ within easy reach of/not far from… and …*

Use comparison and contrast words. ➤➤ See *Graphs* on page 24.

hecking your writing efficiently

Check that you use formal words, e.g. *approximately* not ~~roughly~~; *improved* not ~~got better~~.

Check your spelling.

Check the tenses are correct.

Check singular/plural agreement, especially in processes.

Make sure you haven't written the word *below* in your introduction.

Make sure you answer all parts of the question and link the different charts to each other.

Avoid repetition. If you use the correct reference words and synonyms, this won't happen.

- Check the beginnings of sentences and clauses in model answers. Practise using these
- Use a wide range of structures. It is easy to slip into writing sentences that just follow the basic pattern of *Subject/Verb/Object*.
- Use connecting words and form complex sentences, i.e. sentences with two or more clauses.
- Describe general trends and support what you say with specific data from the chart.
- Plan the steps you are going to take before you go in to the exam: analyse data; draw general conclusions; order; state and then quote specific data.
- ➤➤ See also *Checking your writing efficiently* for *Task 2*, page 41.

Task 2

Golden rules

- Use the question to help you organize your answer.
- Check the general topic of the question, usually: a problem, a point of view or a statement with two opposing views.
- Check how many parts there are to the question.
- Make a brief plan. Use the focus points in the question.
- Plan to write about five paragraphs. Keep this plan in mind:

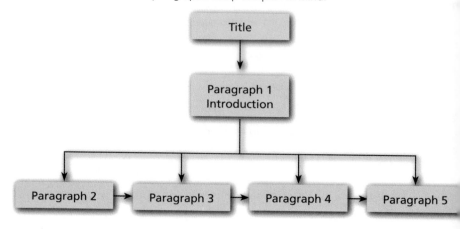

Make very brief notes about what you are going to write for each paragraph – one idea for each paragraph is enough.

Aim to write around 270 words.

Work out how many lines 250 words are in your handwriting, e.g. if you write about ten words per line, then you will need to produce at least 25 lines.

Spend no more than five minutes analysing the question and planning.

Analysing the essay questions and understanding the rubric

Prepare for understanding the questions in Task 2 by looking at the various books available.

Familiarize yourself with the basic structure of the essay question and the rubric.

The essay question usually contains a statement which describes a general situation followed by specific points to write about.

The general statement can present a problem, e.g. *Stress in modern life is increasing.* This may then be followed by questions like *What do you think are the main causes of this? What possible solutions can you suggest?*

Your answer should then be organized around the main causes and then the suggested solutions. In each you case you need to give reasons and support with examples. Remember that you also need to give your opinion.

The organization of the question shows you the organization of your essay. Do not try to contradict it or to be overly clever.

Try to analyse questions by concentrating first on the organizing or words [*causes, effects, solutions*, etc] that are contained in the question.

Make lists of the common words used. Look at Reading, *Matching sentences/phrases to paragraphs* page 14 and compare the words used there.

If you are asked to give your opinion about a point of view, the common instructions used are: To what extent do you agree [or disagree]? How far do you agree [or disagree]? What is your opinion? Note that these may be combined with questions about causes etc.

Note that when you are asked just *To what extent do you agree?* It means that you can disagree!

How to write the introduction

- Keep the introduction short.

- Write no more than two or three sentences – about 30 words.

- Connect your introduction and title. Write a general statement relating to the topic. Then write a sentence which contains the parts of the questions you are asked about: ... *factors contributing to* ... etc.

- Where you can, use synonyms to rephrase the question.

- Cross out any notes in the plan you made.

- Ignore what other people are doing in the examination room.

- Remember that quality is better than quantity. Do not panic if other people are writing more than you.

How to write a paragraph

- Write in stages.

- To connect the paragraph to the introduction, write a statement with a focus word, e.g. *The main cause/factor is* ... Alternatively, you can just state the cause or begin to explain the situation.

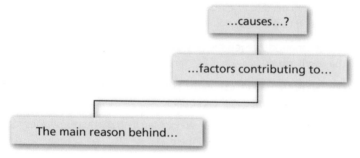

- As a rough guide, write about 75/80 words for each paragraph – about 7/8 lines if you write 10 words per line.

- Mark this on the answer sheet and write towards this mark. Repeat this for the subsequent paragraphs.

- As you write, use a pencil, but try not to rub out corrections or changes, as this wastes a lot of time. You also stop the thread of your writing. Cross out any changes with one line. Write above if you have space. Only rub out the text you want to change if you don't have space to write above.

How to organize a paragraph

Improve your organization and you will make fewer mistakes. You then have more time to concentrate on the grammar, vocabulary and spelling.

Have an aim of how much you want to write for each paragraph.

For 75/80 words, aim to write about four to seven sentences of varying length.

Make sure each paragraph is connected with the previous one, as you are marked according to how you organize each paragraph.

You only need to use a limited range of sentence/clause types to write effectively. Here is a list of the most common types of sentences and clauses you can use to guide you as you write:

- focus statement
- explanation
- general example
- specific example
- result
- reason
- proposal
- advantage
- possibility
- probability
- measure
- condition

- contrast
- additional information
- additional information
- opinion
- fact
- improbability
- improbability
- cause
- effect
- consequence
- purpose/aim

- These types of sentences/clauses fit together in common combinations. For example, what would you write after a *measure* sentence? You could write a *result* or a *reason* sentence.

- Think about how you can combine two or more within sentences and as separate sentences. Don't think about the grammar or vocabulary. Think about an idea and then what functions you would need to explain and support it.

- As you write a paragraph, it will tend to move from general to specific.

How to speed up your writing and make it more flexible

- Start your paragraph with a general statement and then support and explain it.

- Make sure that you do not write a series of general statements.

- When you start to write, develop your main idea by asking yourself questions to guide you. Use the list of functions above. For example:

– What is my focus statement?	*The main measure is …*
– What do I mean by this?	*By this I mean …*
– What is the result of this?	*This will …*
– Can I give a specific result?	*First of all, it will …*
– Can I give a general example?	*For example at the moment, …*
– Can I give a specific example?	*However, … could …*

  How you combine them is up to you, as long as they make sense.

- Practise combining the functions in different ways.

- Widen the range of sentence types that you use. For example, think of sentences in pairs. Then think what would come after the second function in the pair and so on. Practise this until it becomes a fluid and automatic technique.

- The more organized you are in your writing, the more fluent and flexible you will be. So make sure you know and can use a wide range of connections and functions.

- The more organized you are, the fewer mistakes you will make. If you do not have to think about the organization of a question in the exam, you will be able to concentrate on avoiding repetition and expressing your ideas.

- Mark out the end of each paragraph before you write an essay and aim for that point. It helps you to focus your ideas and stops you from rambling.

- Revise efficiently. Take a blank sheet and then write down everything you know about a specific aspect of Writing Task 2: what you know about introductions; what common sentence functions you use; what common connecting words and phrases you know for but, and, so, etc. This will show you what you know and what you don't know. It will help you organize your thoughts and increase your confidence and hence your speed.

- Above all know yourself, your strengths and your limitations and your common mistakes. Then push your limitations and correct your mistakes.

Common mini sequences of functions

- As you become more confident you can build these sequences and as you write and learn to combine in whatever way suits you.

  - measure/result/reason; general example; specific example

- condition (*if/unless*); result; real example
- problem; cause; solution; reason; general and specific example
- opinion; explanation; reason; general example; specific example; my opinion

• Try and think about these sequences without writing them down. Try to combine and recombine.

• Developing your flexibility helps develop the fluency in connecting text and prevents over-generalizing.

• The following checklists are only guidelines and can be adapted in many different ways. You can combine information in endless different ways.

• You can take parts from one checklist and add them to another.

Checklist 1	Checklist 2
statement/focus explanation example reason example result conclusion	statement/focus – specific measure result explanation by examples real example – example of what is already happening somewhere now hypothetical example – example of what you think could happen if the measure were adopted conclusion

Checklist 3: Measure	Checklist 4: Cause/effect
statement/focus – specific measure general result/benefit specific result/benefit accompanying result reservation: *Having said that however, …* additional evidence/reason general conclusion – *So …* own conclusion – *Nevertheless …*	statement/focus – problem explanation by examples effect 1 effect 2 solution: real example – example of what is already happening somewhere now solution: hypothetical example – example of what you think could happen conclusion

How to express your opinion

- There are many ways to express your opinion. If you find it difficult, use the frame below to check and guide.

- Practise writing your own statements of opinion. Then practise supporting them. Use *reasons, results, explanation, contrast, effect, condition,* etc.

- Each time you write a sentence, qualify what you have said.

Checklist 5: Opinion

state your opinion about a situation/problem

explanation – general example: *Every year/In many countries ..., In the past ..., Now ...,* etc.

specific example: *for example,* etc.

specific example: *moreover,* etc.

suggestion: *should/could ...*

counterargument: *However, some people ...*

restate opinion: *Nevertheless, I feel ...*

Opinion expressions

I think/feel/ believe ...

Personally I feel ...

As far as I am concerned, ...

From my point of view, ...

Don't overuse these. Make a statement of opinion.

How to link your sentences

- Below are common words and phrases you know, but which you often forget to use when linking your writing. Check how they are used.

- Match the expressions below with the function checklist. ➤➤ See *How to organize a paragraph* on page 35.

- While practising for the exam, try to use these expressions.

- Before you write and before the exam, read through the expressions again.

- Avoid overusing connecting words, especially too many addition words.

- Revision tip: On a blank sheet of paper, write *addition, comparison,* etc. at the top of the page and then list the words you remember. Check against the list on page 39.

Addition

- Adverbs: *moreover, what is more, furthermore, further, in addition.(to that), additionally, likewise, similarly, besides, equally, as well as, also, on top of that*
- Conjunctions: *and, which/that/whose,* etc. for explanation/adding additional information

Comparison

➤➤ See *Task 1, How to compare and contrast* on page 26.

Condition

- Conjunctions: *if, unless, whether, on condition that, provided that supposing, as/so long as, otherwise*

Examples

- Adverbs: *for example, for instance, such as, as, like*
- Expressions: *take ... for example, a (very) good example/the best example, in many countries/every year/now/in the past,* etc.

Reason/Cause

- Conjunctions: *because, as, since, for*
- *-ing* (present) ... *knowing I'd be late, ...*
- *-ed* (past) ... *warned about the problem ...*

Concession and contrast

- Adverbs: *however, nevertheless, though, even so, but, (and) yet*
- Conjunctions: *although, even though, though, while*
- Prepositions: *despite/in spite of (the fact that)*

Result

- Adverbs: *as a result, as a consequence, consequently, accordingly, therefore, so, on that account, for that reason*
- Conjunctions: *and, so, so that, so + adjective that*
- Other forms: *-ing, which ... this will ...*

Manner

- Conjunctions: *as, as if*

Time

- Conjunctions: *as, as soon as, after, before, since, until when, whenever*

Purpose

- Adverbs: *so*

- Conjunctions: *so, so that, to, in order (not) to, in order that, so as (not) to*

Making generalizations

- Adverbs: *Generally speaking, overall, on the whole, in general, by and large*

Conclusion

- Adverbs: *hence, thus, therefore, consequently*

- Explanation: *by this I mean, which, this*

• Practise making your own checklists.

General writing hints

Writing in English follows some basic principles:

• The basic pattern of an English sentence is: *Subject/Verb/Object.*

• The connecting and reference words generally come at the beginning of the sentences and/or clauses: words like *moreover/he/they/such/this/these/another measure is,* etc.

• English sentences are organized around the principle of old and new information. The reference words refer to the old information and the new idea in the sentence is generally at the end. For example: *An old man entered a shop. The shop had a wide range of food. The food ....* Sometimes the structure is reversed for emphasis. Compare: *Another measure is educating the general public.* (old/new information) with: *Educating the general public is another measure.* (new/old information). The impersonal phrase: *There is/are,* is used to introduce new ideas: *There will be many implications if this policy is introduced.*

• Always check your work as you write. Look backwards as well as forwards.

• Remember what you bring to the writing when you do the exam. Your mind is not a blank sheet!

hecking your writing efficiently

Read this section *before* and *after* you write and keep it in mind.

Leave yourself 3–5 minutes to check your writing.

Be aware of the mistakes you usually make and look out for these. It can make a difference of a score band!

As it is difficult to check for all mistakes at one time, check for one type of mistake at a time.

Check your spelling first. Scan the text backwards rather than forwards. Alternatively scan at random, jumping from one paragraph to another. You will see mistakes quicker as you are not engaging with meaning, but looking at word pictures. You may not spot all the mistakes, but you will get quite a few.

Scan quickly the beginning of each sentence and the beginning of each paragraph. Check if the linking words, the reference words or synonyms you use are correct.

Check the verbs – tense? singular/plural agreement? correct form of the verb?

Check that your connecting linking words are correct and that you have not repeated any of them.

If you tend to make other mistakes, like misusing the articles, study them and look for them in particular.

Practise so that you can do these all at the same time while going through the text from the beginning.

Listening

Exam summary

- The listening module takes approximately 30 minutes.

- There are four separate sections. You hear each section once only.

  - Section one is a conversation between two people on a general or social theme.

  - Section two is a monologue or an interview on a general or social theme.

  - Section three is a conversation between up to four speakers on an educational or training theme.

  - Section four is a talk or lecture on a theme of general academic interest.

- There are usually 40 questions. These questions become progressively more difficult.

- The listening, like the reading component is weighted. The standard is the same on each test day. However, to reach a specific band, the number of correct answers required is different in each exam.

Golden rules

- As the listening module of the exam involves listening, reading, hearing and writing skills, learn to use them simultaneously.

- Develop your organizational and prediction skills, and your concentration.

- Practise listening to a wide range of accents.

- Concentrate on the questions one at a time, but be prepared for the next question. Look ahead if you have time.

- Listen to the instructions on the tape as well. A general clue is usually given.

Develop your skills

Use organizational skills

Skim the questions to get a general idea of the listening and at the same time take a note of key words.

Skim the organization of the questions as well as the language. This helps locate answers. ➤➤ See *Labelling plans/maps* on page 55.

As you listen, scan the recording and the questions for organization markers. ➤➤ See *Labelling plans/maps* on page 55.

Be aware of common patterns in questions, words or grammar, etc.

Take note of any:

– sub-headings

– words in bold in the notes

– headings in columns

These are all markers for you to listen for.

Use the information in the questions to help answer other questions.

Do not choose answers that contradict the general sense of the listening.

Use the general information you have about a listening to predict an answer about specific detail. ➤➤ See *Predict and check* on page 44.

Practise checking the sense at random. If you always read in sequence, you see what you want to see.

Make a list of your common mistakes and read the list before and after writing.

Date your homework writing and go back and check the progression and see how mistakes are made.

Be aware of mistakes that are common to students of English with your mother tongue, e.g. articles, the ends of words, countable/uncountable nouns, tenses, relative pronouns, etc.

If you feel confident doing so, check for mistakes and sense at the end of each paragraph. This will also train you to look back as you write rather than just going forward.

Predict and check

- *Predicting* is not *guessing*. You *guess* when you do not think about an answer or when you do not have time to work it out. You *predict* when you use the information you have or know to give an answer – often a general word to match with a specific detail in the recording.

- For gap-fills, where you can't predict, work out the grammar or word patterns. Think about what kind of word (*noun, verb, adjective, adverb*) is required.

- Predict and then match with the listening. Even if your prediction is different, you have something to listen for.

- Use the collocation of words to help you predict. Words fit together to form common phrases.

- Predicting is about using skills you already use in life generally. So use logic, common sense and the organization of information to predict multiple-choice questions, etc.

- Information and ideas, like words, fit together. Use this to predict. ➤➤ See *Writing* page 34 and *Reading* page 14.

- When you predict, always listen to check the answer.

- Practise until you predict automatically. Skim the questions in a section in any test book and predict the answers. Check your answers with the Answer Key.

Concentrate and write

- Concentrate through the whole exam. If you relax, you end up *hearing* what is being said and not *listening*.

- Concentrate while you are writing answers. If you don't listen to the recording, you may miss the thread of the dialogue.

- Use the your organizational skills and prediction to help you focus and concentrate.

- Use the questions to guide you through the recording.

- Practise hearing information on the radio and then consciously listening to it so you get used to *switching on your concentration*.

- Answers are generally straightforward. Do not expect anything extraordinary.

Manage your time

- Use your time efficiently.

- When you have thirty-second silences, use them for skimming and scanning the questions or checking your answers.

- If you are confident of your answers, use checking time to look ahead.

- As you listen, use the time between answers to skim/scan ahead.

Be speedy and efficient

- Change your skills between sections automatically as required and be decisive. This adds to your speed and efficiency.

- Skim and scan the text at speed and with confidence. ➤➤ See *Reading* pages 7–10.

- If you miss a question, leave it and go to the next one. It is better to miss one question than a whole section.

Paraphrase

- Always look out for synonyms.

- Understanding paraphrasing and different synonyms is about building your vocabulary.

- Remember that you cannot and do not have to know everything. However, you do need to know enough to be able to work out the meanings of words and phrases.

- The more you are comfortable with the words that you do know, the more it will be easier to understand and analyse new words. So even repeating listenings that you have heard before will help to build up your vocabulary range.

- Speaking and reading will also help build your vocabulary for listening.

- It is easy to become obsessed with learning individual words and to forget about their meaning.

- Where possible, limit yourself to learning about five to ten words a day. You will then probably pick up a lot more!

- When working out words and phrases you don't know, use the information in the question and the recording to predict meaning and any answers.

Types of questions

Completing notes

- Look at any general heading on the form/notes to be completed.

- Skim all the questions in the section to get a general idea.

- In Section 1, avoid making any mistakes if you want a good grade. You can easily make mistakes here as this section appears easy and so concentration lapses.

- Remember this section tests for specific detail: *basic words, times, (street) names, numbers*, etc.

- Check the example as this gives you a general idea and a starting point.

- Look at the questions together rather than each one in isolation.

- Check the grammar of the gaps and check the word limit. Then try to predict an answer with a general word.

- Be familiar with numbers and check your spelling. Know the numbers that cause you problems personally.

- Numbers are usually said in groups of two or three.

- Practise saying or listening to numbers in a sequence rather than separately.

- Use any subheadings in the chart/diagram as key words when you listen.

- Avoid over-marking the text.

- Know the pronunciation of the alphabet letters individually and together.

- You may have to complete sentences using items from a list. Make sure you copy the spelling correctly.

- Skim the headings and narrow the grammar/meaning down so you can predict a general answer to fill any gaps.

- One question in a section can help you answer another.

- If the notes are later in the test, they are more difficult.

Short answer questions

- Skim the questions to get a general idea and look at any examples that are listed with the questions. The questions sometimes require two answers or the answers are part of a short list.

- Check for examples which help you with the grammar of the answer. For example: *What types of sports does the speaker mention?*: <u>tennis</u>; _____; _____.

- Look for the organizing words like *types, factors, places, causes*, etc. in the questions.

- Look at these types of organizing words in writing and reading.

Tables

- Check the general heading and the headings of each column. These organize the listening for you, as they guide you through the recording. You can use them to scan the recording.

- Check the word limit and what type of answer is required.

- Check the other words in the columns where the gaps are. They will give an example of what type of word is required.

- Follow patterns of grammar, type of word, number of words, etc. within each column. If all the other items in a column are only one word, then the answer may be the same.

Multiple-choice questions

- ▶▶ See *Reading* page 15 for hints on multiple-choice questions in the reading section. These apply here too.

- Use the questions to help you predict what you will hear.

- Always look at the example as it will give a starting point and a clue to where you are beginning.

- You can get a very good idea of the content of the dialogue from the stem and the alternatives.

- Use logic, your knowledge of the world, common sense, and the other questions for the section to predict your answer. Then check your answer as you listen.

- As in the reading, multiple-choice questions become more difficult as you progress through the test.

- The questions change from facts to actions and then to general idea.

Types of multiple-choice questions

The multiple-choice questions may vary in presentation.

- The question stem can be:
  - a sentence that requires completion
  - a question.
- A more complex variation is where the stem asks you what is *not* included or is *against* an idea. This could be either as a statement for completion or an answer to a question.
- You can also be asked to select *two advantages*, etc. from a list of five items.

The importance of analysing questions

- Pay particular attention to analysing the stem and analysing multiple-choice questions as you prepare for the exam. The techniques involved are very similar to those described for the reading.
- However, for listening you need to be much faster as obviously once the recording has moved in you can become confused. Remember that if you miss an answer, move on.
- The best skill you can develop overcome this is being organized and flexible.
- As you prepare for the exam, study multiple-choice question types carefully. Make sure you are prepared for the progression of difficulty in meaning as you move from section to section.
- An efficient technique is to look at the questions and answers. Work out why the answer is correct without looking at the tapescript or listening to the recording.
- Look for patterns in the alternatives and see how the wrong answers are created. At the beginning of the test the questions are often short simple items. The wrong answers can include items that are mentioned in the recording or may be not given. The items will probably fit within a group, e.g. *a sandwich, a hot snack, a salad, a dessert.*
- This will show you how the questions are created and how the questioning is organized.
- This technique applies to all aspects of the exam, but especially listening and reading.
- When you have finished your analysis, listen to a recording. If necessary, do the same exercises again and again until you feel comfortable with answering the questions.
- Then when you come to questions you have never heard before you will have a stronger foundation.
- As a result you will feel more relaxed about the exam as your understanding and speed increase.

- When you have finished, make notes about what you know regarding multiple-choice questions or other questions you are studying. Then check them with books etc. Keep your notes and try to write them out again later on a blank sheet.

- Turn them into a checklist for each type of question.

- Remember learning a language is like going to the gym, the brain needs exercise - repeated exercise for the body to develop.

- Enjoy exercising!

Summaries

- For this type of question think about:
  - prediction
  - organization
  - general gist from skimming
  - scanning for key words
  - logic and common sense.

- A summary can be a whole section with ten gaps. Such summaries are usually suitable for monologues. As they are slightly more complex, they occur in Section 3/Section 4.

- Look for the general heading of the summary and skim any other general headings.

- Skim all the subheadings quickly. Each subheading usually has a list of bullet points after it. The subheadings tell you about the organization of the monologue or dialogue and summarize the detail.

- Underline words to listen for and words to help you understand meaning.

- Check the items in the summary. Skim very quickly as you may have only one 30 second silence at the beginning.

- If you do not have time to skim and prepare for the whole recording, look first at the main heading, then the subheadings and finally at the specific detail of as many of the items as you can.

- Skim one group of items ahead as you listen. Trying to take the whole summary in at one time can confuse you. Use the headings to guide you through the listening.

- Predict the grammar and general type of word you are looking for and then match as you listen.

- Always check for organizing words, e.g. *areas*, *impact*, *benefits* and pay particular attention to collocations. The same applies to short summaries.

Completing sentences

• Follow the previous hints on organization and prediction.

• Check for collocations. ➤➤ See *Reading, Completing Sentences,* page 17.

• Skim the questions and predict.

• In some cases, two answers are required. You have to get both correct to get a mark, but the order in which you write them is not important.

• Remember to check the word limit and the grammar. If the instructions refer to a number, then at least one of the answers is likely to be a number.

Labelling plans/maps

• Skim the diagram to get a general idea and find a reference point for starting.

• Look first for general names on the map/plan like *entrance, courtyard, river* and then any specific items like those you have to name, e.g, types of buildings.

• Look at the gaps to be filled and predict the type of word/s needed.

• To negotiate maps and plans you will need to understand directions.

• Common direction words to think of: *on the left/right; on the top left/right of ...; to my/our/your left/ right; in the bottom/top right/left (hand) corner opposite ...; next/ adjacent to ...; beside ...; on the far/other side of; in front of; over there,* etc.

• Listen for the word *now.* It is used to indicate the end of one piece of information and the beginning of another. Phrases like: *You go (down) to ... and then ...* are also common.

• You may also have to choose items from a list of names with a plan and write down a letter.

abelling a diagram/bar chart/graph

- Follow the instructions for completing sentences on page 50. Remember to check word limit and grammar.

- ➤➤ See *Writing, Task 1*, pages 39–40 for useful language.

- Analyse the chart and make sure you know the values of the items so you can match numbers to the names in the recording.

  Use any items given to find patterns when you listen.

- Listen for markers in the recording. The names on the graphs may be summaries of ideas in the text, so listen for meaning and paraphrase.

Matching

- Matching can take several forms. It can include matching items with a graph/chart or map/diagram. ➤➤ See *Labelling plans/maps* on page 50.

- You can be asked to evaluate items like people, books, places, etc using a scale with up to seven values ranging from *Bad* to *Very good*, for example, or *Don't read* to *Highly recommended*.

- Look at the first and last in the range on the scale first, and then skim the full range.

- As you listen, focus on one item to be evaluated, while looking at the scale.

- Break up the task into individual pieces of information.

- Be ready to move on from one piece of information to the next one on the list.

- Remember that the questions guide you.

- Be organized and decisive.

Completing the answer sheet

- Use the ten minutes to transfer the answers you have at the end of the listening exam fully.

- Use your time effectively and efficiently.

- It is easy just to be satisfied that you are finished and then remember that you have left something out. Check to the last possible moment.

- Use a pencil to complete the answer sheet and avoid writing outside the space for the answer.

- Be careful with simple answers because this is where many mistakes are made. Generally, we all concentrate on the more difficult questions and relax with the easy ones.

- Keep your concentration up throughout the test and especially when you are transferring answers.

- Think as you transfer, don't just copy words.

- Always be aware of the time.

- Be very careful as you transfer the answers, even if they seem very straightforward. It is easy to make careless mistakes.

- Check spelling, grammar and the word limit.

- Make sure you do not repeat words from the stem.

- Make sure the answers are in the correct space. Concentrate as you write them in; don't just copy without thinking.

- Remember that one wrong mark can affect your grade.

- When you have completed the sheet, check everything quickly or at least do a quick random check.

- Check using the questions if you have time.

- Check sequences of multiple choice answers to make sure they are in order.

- Be careful about changing answers; check any answer against the information in the question booklet.

- If at this stage there are any gaps in the answers, guess if you cannot predict, especially if the answers are multiple-choice questions or letters.

Speaking

Exam summary

- The speaking module takes 11–14 minutes.
- There are three sections.
  - Part 1 (4–5 minutes) is for the Examiner to introduce him/herself and ask you questions about yourself.
  - Part 2 (3–4 minutes) is for you to prepare and give a short talk of 1–2 minutes on a given subject.
  - Part 3 (4–5 minutes) is for you and the Examiner to have a discussion linked to the subject from Part 2.
- You will be assessed on your:
  - fluency and coherence
  - vocabulary
  - range of grammar and accuracy
  - pronunciation.

Golden rules

Speak as much English as you can.

Prepare yourself for the exam by knowing what is involved.

You need to sound natural and not as if you have learnt answers by heart. Be spontaneous and relevant.

Do not be put off by the tape recorder in the room. It is there to help you not the Examiner!

Be positive. The exam is nearly over, so smile and breathe evenly.

Remember that the adrenaline produced by your nervous feelings actually helps you to perform better.

Use a wide range of vocabulary. People generally use less than they know when they speak. Practise to activate what you know.

- Concentrate generally on what you are saying rather than being accurate. You will then make fewer mistakes.

- Practise speaking *clearly*. This does not mean *slowly*, but *naturally* and *evenly*.

How to be fluent
- Concentrate on the planning and organization. These help you to control your nerves and to be fluent. If you go into the exam unprepared, it will make you nervous.

- Concentrate only on the part you are doing. Forget about the other parts of the exam.

Eye contact
- Keep eye contact with the Examiner, even if he/she looks away or makes notes. If you do not usually maintain eye contact in your culture, practise speaking while keeping eye contact before the exam.

- If the Examiner is writing, looking away or not smiling, this does not mean that you are doing badly. It just means the Examiner is doing his/her job.

Part 1: Introduction and interview
- Remember that the Examiner is just like your teacher. In fact, Examiners are usually teachers, so they are aware of how you feel, because their own students feel the same!

- The Examiner has a set of questions. Answer the questions without trying to repeat the whole question in your answer:
  What's the most interesting building in your home town?
  Do not reply: ~~The most interesting place in … is …~~
  Say: *It's …*

- State your answer and then expand, if possible.
  I/Many people find it fascinating, because …

- Try to use synonyms of the words used by the Examiner. If you can't, don't interrupt your fluency, just say what you can.

- The topics are usually familiar topics and the Examiner asks you about yourself. Try to give examples and create ideas. Do not say: ~~I don't know.~~

You might be asked about:

- a place or a hobby

- your daily routine

- your interests

- places in your country

- special foods/events in your country.

The questions are designed to *encourage* you to talk. They are not new or unpredictable.

Part 2: Individual long turn

• The topics on the task card are about a book, film, television programme, clothes, piece of music, object, place you like, special journey, special day, people you like or who have influenced you or a skill you have learned, etc.

• Use the time to plan. A common criticism of candidates is that they do not plan. You are *not* impressing the Examiner if you start immediately without planning, whatever your level. Make a brief written plan, as it helps to keep you on the subject and stops you from wandering away from the points you are asked about.

• If your talk is not organized, you will lose marks.

• Remember you are being checked on your fluency and coherence. Coherence involves following a logical and clear argument.

Remember that being relevant is as important being fluent.

• When candidates do not plan, they tend to describe the general aspect of the question rather than the specific parts.

• Be aware how much you can say in two minutes maximum. You will probably only be able to say between 200–250 words.

• Make sure what you say is natural and do not sound as if you have learnt something by heart. It will affect your score.

Remember the Examiner will know if you are doing the task properly or not.

Planning and making notes

- Write notes not sentences. The task card asks you to describe a place, etc. and then to give reasons for your choice. For each point, write only one or two words for each prompt. In total you should have no more than 10–20 words.

- Write the points in a vertical list and in order. It is easier to see them this way.

- Draw a line between the words relating to the description and the explanation. It will make it clearer for you as you speak.

- As you speak, refer to the list to organize your answer. This should ensure that you answer all parts of the task.

- Use nouns, verbs, adverbs and adjectives for your notes.

- Do not learn your notes or full answers by heart and then repeat them word for word in the exam quickly. This sounds artificial and affects your score.

- Think about connecting words/phrases that will guide you as you speak, but don't write them in the notes.

Organization

- Like the other parts of the test, the Speaking tests your ability to organize what you say. Good organization improves your fluency and coherence and reduces your mistakes.

- Practise making notes and using them to help you speak.

- Learn to build what you say around the prompts on the card and your notes.

- Record yourself; even write your answer down to see how much you need to say.

- Do not learn what you have written by heart, but do learn words and phrases that prompt and guide you.

ompt words for Part 2

Use prompt words to guide you rather than leaning whole topics.

Here are some introductory prompt phrases:

- *I'd like to talk about …*
- *I'm going to talk about/describe how to …*
- *I want to talk about …*
- *What I'd like to talk about is …*

Here are some phrases to talk about background detail:

- Place: *It is near …*
- Name: *A _____ called/which is called …*
- Location: *_____ is situated … on the shores of/on the edge of …*
- Time: *It took place …/It happened …*
- Recent time: *It has been going on …/I have known …*
- How: *First of all, you prepare …; then … is prepared …*

Here are some words and phrases to help develop your theme:

- *First of all, …/Secondly, …*
- *and also/as well as/what's more/moreover*
- *Another thing is…/Another reason I …/Another reason why I …/Another reason behind my decision to …*
- *because/since/as*
- *And why do I like it so much? Well, it …*

Here are some words and phrases to talk about things you like:

- *I like/enjoy something/doing something.*
- *I like … more than anything else.*
- *I like … the most.*
- *I love something/doing something …*

- – ... *appeals to me, because ...*
- – *I take get (a lot of) pleasure out of ...*
- – *I am fond of ...*

- Here are some words and phrases to state that something made an impression on you

  - – ... *made an impression on me.*
  - – ... *influenced me.*
  - – ... *had an (enormous) impact on me.*
  - – ... *affected me.*
  - – ... *had an effect on me.*
  - – ... *seems to have a had lasting effect on me.*
  - – ... *brought home to me ...*
  - – ... *changed the way I look at things.*
  - – ... *moved me.*
  - – ... *impressed me.*
  - – ... *touched me deeply.*
  - – ... *disturbed me.*

- Use synonyms of words in the task card.

  - – **benefits**: *advantages, positive aspects*
  - – **ways**: *measures, steps, courses of action, solutions*
  - – **causes**: *reasons behind*
  - – **effects**: *consequences, repercussions, results*
  - – **developments**: *changes*
  - – **example**: *instance, good example, best example*

- Collect your own examples of synonyms.

- As you think about and give your talk, be prepared for questions to connect what you have said in Part 2 to lead into Part 3.

art 3: Two-way discussion

Listen carefully to the Examiner's questions.

Try to be fluent and only correct yourself if it is easy to do so. Don't focus on your mistakes.

Concentrate on the organization and being coherent.

Remember the Examiner asks you a range of questions to *encourage* you to speak.

You need to go into greater depth to explain your opinion, give reasons and speculate about the future.

To stop yourself from panicking about Part 3, think how long it lasts; how many questions the Examiner can ask you (six to eight); and the nature of the questions.

The questions will be open questions, for example:

- *What kind(s)/sort(s)/type(s)/benefit(s)/effect(s) of ... are there?*

- *What kinds of things ...?*

- *What changes/advantages/disadvantages/differences/ways ...?*

- *Why do you think ...?*

- *How important/useful/beneficial/essential ...?*

- *How does ...?*

- (A statement) *Why do you think this is?*

- *What will happen in the future?*

- *Can you give me some examples?*

- *Do you think ...? Why?*

- *What is the role of ...?*

The Examiner can invite you to comment by asking: *What about...?*

Keep to the topic. Think of your answer as the Examiner is speaking.

ompts to help you begin and develop your answers

If you don't understand the Examiner's question, tell him/her or ask him/her to repeat it. There is no point answering a question you do not understand.

Make sure that your answer fits the Examiner's question.

- A memorized response to something similar you have learnt is not suitable. However, prepare some prompts for yourself so that you can get yourself talking. These prompt give you a few seconds to think and organize what you want to say.

- Remember that the Examiners are not checking whether you are telling the truth, but your ability to speak English.

- The Examiner introduces a general topic and then asks you a question about a specific aspect.

- When the Examiner asks you a question, listen for words you can build your answer around: *What do you think the benefits of being able to speak more than one language are?* Obviously, you need to speak about the *benefits*. When you answer, us a paraphrase: *advantages/positive aspects* or … *is beneficial.*

- Put your list into an order: *The main advantage, I think, is…* and give one or more reasons: … *because … and it …*

- You are taking part in a *two-way* conversation. Allow space for the Examiner to ask yo questions. Don't talk over the Examiner. However, if the Examiner doesn't interrupt yo continue speaking.

- Don't speak fast or slowly, but clearly.

- Organize what you are saying. Don't make just the beginning relevant, but also your supporting evidence. Bear in mind the principles of writing a paragraph.

- Concentrate on the message and the organization rather than your grammar and it w help you to be fluent.

- The Examiner might ask a question that changes direction slightly. Follow his/her lead.

Developing ideas

- When you state something, try to qualify it and expand to support your opinion/reason

  - *The main way/step/measure I think, is to …*

  - *… because this will/can lead to … and also …*

  - *For example, …*

  - *And another way is … I also think/feel/believe … In my opinion/From my point of view …*

- Use, but don't overuse, adding words: *Moreover/What is more*

- If you have time, draw a conclusion: … *and therefore …*

You can vary the response in any way you like as long as it fits and is relevant.

The Examiner might ask an unexpected question for you to comment on:
What about...? Agree or disagree: *That is possible, but I think ...* and give your reasons.

Use words and phrases to state different sides of an argument:

- *To some people ... is a downside/drawback/disadvantage, but on balance I think ...*

- *... but/however/nevertheless I ...*

Talk about possible results or consequences: *... and so/therefore ...*

When you are asked to speculate about the future, use: *will/going to/might/could/should.*

reathing

Keep to the subject and try not to speak too fast. Speak and breathe – take shallow breaths.

Break up what you say up into chunks that you can say. Take a shallow breath between each chunk.

Your voice goes up at the same points where you have a comma in writing. You will also go up in the middle of a long sentence maybe once or twice. This indicates to the Examiner that you are continuing to speak and also gives a brief chance to take a shallow breath.

$$\uparrow \qquad\qquad \uparrow$$
The main benefit, I think, is that computers allow students
$$\uparrow$$
to collect a lot of material in one place when they are ...

You linger very slightly on the words *that, students* and *place* and take a very shallow quick breath, before you go on.

Use this breathing technique to break up what you are saying rather than just taking one long breath and running to the end of the sentence.

Practise the technique with a friend and listen to English people speaking. It will help stop you from trying to say everything in one breath.

Tips for IELTS Skills Checklists

How to use the checklists

- Do not write in the checklists but make a number of copies so that you can use them repeatedly.

- Keep some spare copies at the back of the book.

- Each time you do an exercise on you own or in a class, skim the relevant checklist.

- When you have finished, check your performance against the list.

- Circle the number 1-9 (where 9 is the highest). The assessment will help you see the IELTS Score Band you are likely to be in.

- Be realistic about your self-assessment and check it with friends and even a teacher.

- Try to make yourself write notes however brief and compare them as you go along.

- Date and keep a copy so you can monitor your own development.

- If you are studying with a friend compare your assessment and use the assessments to discuss your strengths and weaknesses.

- Make notes when you can about your performance.

- Make similar lists of your own for specific aspects of the exam, like paragraph heading etc.

Just before the exam

- Use the checklists for last minute revision. Pay attention to the notes you made.

- Refer to the relevant tips in the book.

Reading Skills Checklist Date: _____	Circle 1 – 9	Notes on progress
1 I skim and analyse questions at speed.	1 2 3 4 5 6 7 8 9	
2 I skim the instructions to check for changes.	1 2 3 4 5 6 7 8 9	
3 I use the questions to summarize the text.	1 2 3 4 5 6 7 8 9	
4 I see the relationship between questions.	1 2 3 4 5 6 7 8 9	
5 I leave questions I can't do and come back again.	1 2 3 4 5 6 7 8 9	
6 I am fast and accurate.	1 2 3 4 5 6 7 8 9	
7 I can skim the text easily.	1 2 3 4 5 6 7 8 9	
8 I can scan the text easily.	1 2 3 4 5 6 7 8 9	
9 I can move around a text with ease.	1 2 3 4 5 6 7 8 9	
10 I can ignore words I don't know.	1 2 3 4 5 6 7 8 9	
11 I predict as I skim/ scan and check my answers.	1 2 3 4 5 6 7 8 9	
12 I manage my time efficiently.	1 2 3 4 5 6 7 8 9	
13 I complete the Answer Sheet accurately.	1 2 3 4 5 6 7 8 9	

Task 1 Writing Skills Checklist Date: _____	Circle 1 – 9	Notes on progress
1 I skim the question and diagram efficiently.	1 2 3 4 5 6 7 8 9	
2 I plan my answer.	1 2 3 4 5 6 7 8 9	
3 I rephrase the question.	1 2 3 4 5 6 7 8 9	
4 I check for mistakes efficiently: spelling; grammar; prepositions; collocations repetition; singular/plural; tenses; countable/uncountable nouns; my common mistakes.	1 2 3 4 5 6 7 8 9	
5 I organize my writing and use paragraphs.	1 2 3 4 5 6 7 8 9	
6 I write at least 150 words.	1 2 3 4 5 6 7 8 9	
7 I summarize the information in diagram(s), report the main features and support with specific data.	1 2 3 4 5 6 7 8 9	
8 I use a wide range of grammar and vocabulary.	1 2 3 4 5 6 7 8 9	
9 I make relevant comparisons.	1 2 3 4 5 6 7 8 9	
10 I check connections in the text.	1 2 3 4 5 6 7 8 9	
11 I look back at what I have written as I write.	1 2 3 4 5 6 7 8 9	
12 I write a conclusion.	1 2 3 4 5 6 7 8 9	

Task 2 Writing Skills Checklist Date: _____	Circle 1 – 9	Notes on progress
1 I analyse the question carefully.	1 2 3 4 5 6 7 8 9	
2 I plan my answer.	1 2 3 4 5 6 7 8 9	
3 I rephrase the question.	1 2 3 4 5 6 7 8 9	
4 I check for mistakes efficiently: spelling and grammar; prepositions; collocations; repetition; singular/plural; tenses; countable/uncountable nouns; my common mistakes.	1 2 3 4 5 6 7 8 9	
5 I manage my time efficiently.	1 2 3 4 5 6 7 8 9	
6 I organize my writing and use paragraphs.	1 2 3 4 5 6 7 8 9	
7 I write at least 250 words.	1 2 3 4 5 6 7 8 9	
8 I use complex sentences and a range of functions, e.g. reasons and examples.	1 2 3 4 5 6 7 8 9	
9 I do not over-generalize.	1 2 3 4 5 6 7 8 9	
10 I use a wide range of grammar and vocabulary.	1 2 3 4 5 6 7 8 9	
11 I use appropriate connections.	1 2 3 4 5 6 7 8 9	
12 I look back at what I have written as I write.	1 2 3 4 5 6 7 8 9	
13 I write a conclusion.	1 2 3 4 5 6 7 8 9	

Listening Skills Checklist Date: _____	Circle 1 – 9	Notes on progress
1 I can listen, read and write simultaneously.	1 2 3 4 5 6 7 8 9	
2 I check the grammar of questions and predict the answer.	1 2 3 4 5 6 7 8 9	
3 I know how to deal with all types of questions.	1 2 3 4 5 6 7 8 9	
4 I see relationships between questions.	1 2 3 4 5 6 7 8 9	
5 I concentrate all the time. So I *listen* to the recording, rather than just *hear*.	1 2 3 4 5 6 7 8 9	
6 I find dialogues easy to listen to.	1 2 3 4 5 6 7 8 9	
7 I find monologues easy to listen to.	1 2 3 4 5 6 7 8 9	
8 I use the questions to help me understand the recording.	1 2 3 4 5 6 7 8 9	
9 I can ignore words I don't know.	1 2 3 4 5 6 7 8 9	
10 I manage my time efficiently.	1 2 3 4 5 6 7 8 9	
11 I complete the Answer Sheet carefully.	1 2 3 4 5 6 7 8 9	

Speaking Skills Checklist Date: _____	Circle 1 – 9	Notes on progress
1 I speak fluently.	1 2 3 4 5 6 7 8 9	
2 I speak accurately.	1 2 3 4 5 6 7 8 9	
3 I speak clearly.	1 2 3 4 5 6 7 8 9	
4 I give relevant and appropriate answers.	1 2 3 4 5 6 7 8 9	
5 I manage my time efficiently.	1 2 3 4 5 6 7 8 9	
6 I organize myself well as I speak.	1 2 3 4 5 6 7 8 9	
7 I use a wide range of grammar and vocabulary.	1 2 3 4 5 6 7 8 9	
8 I can use complex sentences and a range of functions, e.g. reasons and examples.	1 2 3 4 5 6 7 8 9	
9 I do not over-generalize.	1 2 3 4 5 6 7 8 9	
10 I can develop an argument.	1 2 3 4 5 6 7 8 9	
11 I use appropriate connections.	1 2 3 4 5 6 7 8 9	
12 I use the correct word and sentence stress and sentence rhythm.	1 2 3 4 5 6 7 8 9	

Tips for IELTS © Macmillan Publishers Limited 2006 **Photocopiable**